BIBLIOGRAPHY DEALING WITH CRIME

Patterson Smith Reprint Series in
Criminology, Law Enforcement, and Social Problems

A listing of publications in the Series *will be found at rear of volume*

Publication No. 103: Patterson Smith Reprint Series in Criminology, Law Enforcement, and Social Problems

A CONTRIBUTION TOWARDS A BIBLIOGRAPHY DEALING WITH CRIME AND COGNATE SUBJECTS

By SIR JOHN CUMMING

Third Edition
Reprinted with Corrections

MONTCLAIR, N. J. : PATTERSON SMITH : 1970

Third edition originally published 1935
Reprinted 1970
by special arrangement with
The Receiver for the Metropolitan Police District,
New Scotland Yard, London
Patterson Smith Publishing Corporation
Montclair, New Jersey 07042

SBN 87585–103–7

Library of Congress Catalog Card Number: 71–108220

This book is printed on three-hundred-year acid-free paper.

PREFACE.

THE first and second editions of this bibliography concerning Crime and several cognate subjects were prepared in 1914 and in 1916 at a time when the present compiler held an administrative post in India dealing with Police and Prisons. It was primarily intended for the use of the libraries of two Provincial Police Colleges in India. Within a further twenty years a great deal more material has been collected: during this period, especially the second half, there has been a large output of criminological literature, and an increasing interest taken by the public in the prevention and detection of crime and in the humanitarian treatment of the criminal. From 1928 to 1930 the compiler had also experience as the founding editor of "*The Police Journal*", and more recently has assisted in regard to the formation of a library at the Metropolitan Police College inaugurated in 1934. The time seems clearly opportune for a new edition. This third edition has accordingly been prepared and placed at the disposal of the Secretary of State for Home Affairs, who has kindly consented to its being printed and published by the Receiver for the Metropolitan Police District.

Criminology has been held to include the whole problem of crime and its treatment in human society. The subject is vast and world wide, co-extensive with the frailty of human nature; therefore, some selection has to be made. A complete bibliography trenches on the one hand on the domain of psychology, and on the other on the domain of law: it overlaps the spheres of the physician, the lawyer, the statesman, and the social worker. In addition to the books published in English within the British Empire, there has been a considerable output of literature published in the United States, as is indicated in Kuhlman's *Guide* (1929) and Culver's *Bibliography* (1934) on p. 88. There is also and extensive literature on the subject in French, German and Italian. Criminal anthropology is the speciality of Italian, and criminal psychology of German publications. Although not professing to be exhaustive, this list of books has now, after a rigorous revision, been made reasonably comprehensive and international, covering in the main a period of fifty years. Pamphlets are generally excluded, but some special items from periodical literature have been inserted. The earlier items are naturally out of print; but this does not detract from their value as sources for the historical study of their respective sections. The standpoint of the compilation, as distinct from bibliographies prepared in the United States of America or on the Continent, is British.

The system of the classification of titles within the sections is mainly analytical; and chronological, not alphabetical, within each sub-section; but the requisite alphabetical reference is furnished by two indexes, one being a subject index combined with a geographical index, and the other an index of authors. The original classification has been revised considerably: there are now over 200 subject headings, dealing with about 1900 titles. Each entry contains, first, the title in italics; followed by the author's name in roman capitals; followed by the imprint, within brackets, of (i) place, (ii) publisher's name and (iii) date. As regards the imprint, where no place of publication is given, it is to be assumed, generally, in the case of books written in English, that it is London. For the purpose of facilitating research pains have been taken to ascertain as far as possible, and to insert, the names of publishers. The arrangement of entries under each subject heading is in the order of date of publication ; thus an easy reference is ensured to the relevant literature in any particular section, showing the development of ideas. There is inevitably some overlapping in the headings. In a few cases certain entries which are applicable to more than one heading are repeated under such headings ; there are also cross references. Explanatory notes are inserted in square brackets.

For help and advice received the compiler would record his grateful acknowledgments to Lord Trenchard, Commissioner of Police of the Metropolis, and Lt.-Col. J. F. C. Carter, Deputy Asst. Commissioner ; to Sir John Moylan, Receiver, and Mr. L. W. Fox, Deputy Receiver, Metropolitan Police ; to Lt.-Col. G. H. R. Halland, Commandant, and Chief Inspector R. Morrish, Metropolitan Police College ; and to Mr. C. H. Putley, Superintendent of Printing, New Scotland Yard.

It is hoped that the collection in its revised form may furnish material for the comparative study of facts and opinions, relating to different periods and to different countries, and may thus be of use to administrative officers of the public services, as well as to students of sociology in its many phases.

London,
August, 1935.

TABLE OF CONTENTS

ABSTRACT

Page

DETAILED CLASSIFICATON
OF
SUBJECT HEADINGS

A. CRIMINOLOGY

B. CRIMINALS AND CRIMINAL CASES

C. HISTORY AND MEMOIRS OF POLICE FORCES (*See also* D.)

D. POLICE ADMINISTRATION (*See also* C.)

E. DETECTION, PRINCIPLES AND METHODS

F. CRIMINAL TRIALS

G. PENOLOGY

H. REFORMATION (*See also* G.)

J. CONNECTED ASSOCIATIONS

K.

EXPLANATORY NOTE

If the author's name is known, consult the *Author Index*, page 97.

If it is desired to ascertain what literature there is on any given subject or with reference to any geographical area, consult the combined *Subject and Geographical Index*, page 91.

The books under each subject or each geographical area will be found arranged in the order of the date of publication.

The author's name will be found after each title.

The place of publication will be found before the name of publisher.

The heading of each subject will be found explained in the *Detailed Classification of Subject headings*, page IX.

Vitia erunt, donec homines.—*Tacitus.*

Nemo repente fuit turpissimus.—*Juvenal.*

Tuta scelera esse possunt: secura non possunt.—*Seneca.*

The annals of criminal jurisprudence exhibit human nature in a variety of positions, at once the most striking, interesting and affecting. They present tragedies of real life, often brightened in their effect by the grossness of the injustice and the malignity of the prejudices which accompany them.—*Burke.*

BIBLIOGRAPHY

DEALING WITH

CRIME AND COGNATE SUBJECTS

A. CRIMINOLOGY

A I — GENERAL

A I 1 — CRIMINOLOGY PROPER. [*See also* 'Criminology Series' (F. Unwin) and 'Modern Criminal Science Series' (Heinemann) in Author Index].

Criminologia, Studio sul delitto, sulle sue Cause e sui Mezzi di Repressione. Raffaele Garofalo, late President of the Court of Appeals of Naples. (Turin, 1890. Tr. by R. W. Millar, Modern Criminal Science Series; Boston, Little, 1911; Heinemann, 1914).

Criminology. Arthur Macdonald. (New York, Funk & Wagnalls, 1893). [Contains bibliography of crime].

Des Principes Sociologiques de la Criminologie. R. de la Grasserie. (Paris, Giard & Brière, 1901).

Fauna Criminal, Estudio de Criminologia practica. E. de P. Alderete-Vilchas. (Madrid, 1904).

The Positive School of Criminology. [Lectures, University of Naples, 1901]. Enrico Ferri [1856-1923]. (Chicago, Kerr, 1906).

La Criminologia. J. Ingegnieros. (Buenos Aires, 1911).

Criminology. M. F. Parmelee. (New York, Macmillan, 1918).

The Principles of Criminology with special reference to their application to India. Sitaram Vandhyopadhyaya. (Calcutta, 1919).

Principles of Criminology. Subrahmania Pillai. (Tagore Law Lectures, 1920; Madras, 1924).

Last Studies in Criminology. [Four cases of miscarriage of justice]. H. B. Irving. (Collins, 1921). [Adolf Beck, Lesurques, La Roncière, Peter Vaux].

Glengarry's Way and other Studies in Criminology. W. Roughead. (Edinburgh, Green, 1922).

Criminology. E. N. Sutherland. (Philadelphia, Lippincott, 1924, 1925).

Crime and the Criminal: an introduction to Criminology. Philip A. Parsons. (New York, Knopf, 1926). [Contains chapter bibliographies].

Criminology and Penology. John Lewis Gillin, Prof. of Sociology, University of Wisconsin. (New York, Century Co., 1926; J. Cape, 1927).

The New Criminology. A consideration of the chemical causation of abnormal behaviour. N. G. Schlapp & E. H. Smith. (New York, Boni & Liveright, 1928).

Criminology. H. Wyndham. (Sixpenny Series; Benn, 1929).

Criminology. FREDERICK E. HAYNES. (McGraw Hill Publications in Sociology; New York, 1930).

Criminology. Art. in 'Encyclopaedia of the Social Sciences,' Vol. IV. HARRY E. BARNES. (Macmillan, 1931). [Has bibliography].

Kriminologie. W. A. WILLEMSE & C. I. RADEMEYER. (Pretoria, 1931).

Inleiding tot de criminologie. W. A. BONGER. (Haarlem, 1932).

Criminology. ROBERT H. GAULT. (Boston, D. C. Heath, 1932; Harrap, 1933).

Criminology. ALBERT MORRIS, Assist. Prof. Social Sciences, Boston, U.S.A. (Social Science Series, Longmans, 1935). [Has bibliography].

A I 2 — PERIODICALS DEVOTED TO CRIMINOLOGY. [*See also* E II 8].

(*a*) ENGLAND

The Howard Journal: a review of modern methods for the prevention and treatment of crime and juvenile delinquency. (London, Howard League; from 1921).

The Medico-Legal and Criminological Review. (London, Baillière; from 1933).

(*b*) EUROPE

BELGIUM

Revue de Droit Pénal et de Criminologie et Archives internationales de médicine légale. (Bruxelles, 55 rue Ducale).

FRANCE

Revue Internationale de Criminalistique. (Lyon, 36-42 Passage de Hotel Dieu; Desvigne).

GERMANY

Archiv für Kriminologie. (Leipzig, Vogel).

SPAIN

Revista espanola de criminologia y psiquiatria forense. (Madrid, Imprunta de Juan Pueys, Luna 29).

(*c*) AMERICA

Journal of the American Institute of Criminal Law and Criminology. (Chicago, Northwestern University Press: quarterly; from 1910).

A II — HISTORY OF CRIME. [*See also* A IV 3].

Crime in England: its Relation, Character and Extent as developed from 1801 to 1848. THOMAS PLINT. (London, Cash, 1851).

A History of Crime in England, illustrating the changes in the progress of Civilization. 2 vols. L. OWEN PIKE. (Smith & Elder, 1873–76).

Crime in England and Wales in the Nineteenth Century: An Historical and Critical Retrospect. WILLIAM HOYLE. (Effingham Wilson, 1876).

Crime and Criminals, 1876-1910. R. F. QUINTON, late Medical Officer, H.M. Prison, Holloway. (Longmans, 1910).

Offences against the State in Roman Law and the Courts which were competent to take cognizance. P. M. SCHIZAS. (London, Univ. of London Press, 1926).

Crime and Custom in Savage Society. [Pt. II. on primitive crime and its punishment]. B. MALINOWSKI. (Intern. Liby. of Psychology; Kegan Paul, 1926).

A III—STUDIES OF CRIME IN GENERAL

A III 1 — GREAT BRITAIN.

An enquiry into the Causes of the late Increase of Robbers, etc., with some proposals for remedying this Growing Evil. H. FIELDING. [The novelist]. (London, A. Millar, 1751).

The Defects of Police, the Cause of Immorality and the Continual Robberies Committed. JONAS HANWAY. (London, 1775).

Treatise on the Police of the Metropolis. DR. P. COLQUHOUN. [Exposed the state of crime in London]. (London, Fry, 1796).

A Letter to the Magistrates of England on the Increase in Crime. SIR JOHN EARDLEY WILMOT. [Lord Chief Justice of the Court of Common Pleas]. (London, 1827).

Religion and Crime. J. M. MORGAN. (Longmans, 1841).

Crime: its Amount, Causes, and Remedies. FREDERICK HILL, late Inspector of Prisons. (Murray, 1853).

Suggestions for the Repression of Crime, in Charges to Grand Juries. M. D. HILL. (London, John W. Parker, 1857).

Crime and Pauperism. W. HOYLE. (Manchester, 1881).

Crime: its Causes and Remedy. L. GORDON RYLANDS. (Unwin, 1888).

War with Crime, being a selection of printed papers on Crime, Reformatories, etc. T. B. BAKER. (Longmans, 1889).

The Problem of Cain: a Study in the treatment of Criminals. W. TRUMBULL, Attorney-at-Law. (London, 1890).

Crime and its Causes. REV. W. D. MORRISON, of H.M. Prison, Wandsworth. (Swan Sonnenschein, 1891, 1902, 1909; Unwin, 1897).

Crime and Common Sense: present judicial inefficiency and direction of improvement. 'INVESTIGATOR' and CAPTAIN ARTHUR ST. JOHN. (London, C. W. Daniel, 1904).

Criminal Responsibility. DR. CHARLES MERCIER. (Clarendon Press, 1905).

The Story of Crime: from the cradle to the grave. H. L. ADAM. (Werner Laurie, 1908).

Education, Personality and Crime. [A practical treatise built up on scientific details dealing with different social problems]. DR. ALBERT WILSON. (Greening, 1908).

Crime and Criminals. R. F. QUINTON. (Longmans, 1910).

Crime and Criminals, being the Jurisprudence of Crime, Medical, Biological and Psychological. C. A. MERCIER [1852–1919]. (University of London Press, 1911, 1918, 1919).

Sidelights on Criminal Matters. JOHN C. GOODWIN. (Hutchinson, 1923).

The Treatment of Crime. [The C.O.P.E.C. Commission Report, Vol. VI. Conference on Christian Politics, Economics and Citizenship]. (Longmans, 1924).

Crime and the Criminal. P. A. PARSONS. (Knopf, 1926).

The Elements of Crime. [Psycho-social Interpretation]. BORIS BRAZOL, formerly Prosecuting Attorney, St. Petersburg Supreme Court. (Oxford University Press, New York Branch, 1928).

A New Way with Crime. [Puts forward alternative methods of treatment]. A. FENNER BROCKWAY. (Williams & Norgate, 1928).

Cain: or the Future of Crime. G. GODWIN. (Kegan Paul, 1928).

The 'Young Person's' Complete Guide to Crime. C. G. L. DU CANN. (Grant Richards & Humphrey Toulmin, 1929).

The Art of Crime. ARTHUR R. L. GARDNER. (P. Allan, 1931).

Education, Crime and Social Progress. WILLIAM C. BAGLEY. (Macmillan, 1931).

The Menace in our Midst. CHRISTMAS HUMPHREYS. (Chapman & Hall, 1932).

Crime, Law and Social Science. JEROME MICHAEL and MORTIMER ADLER. (Intern. Liby. of Psychology, etc.; Kegan Paul, 1933).

The Lawbreaker : a critical Study of the modern treatment of crime. E. ROY CALVERT and THEODORA CALVERT. (Routledge, 1933).

Crime and Humane Ethics. CARL HEATH. (Allenson, 1934).

Movies, Delinquency and Crime. HERBERT BLUMER and PHILIP M. HAUSER. (New York; Macmillan, 1934).

A III 2 — EUROPE.

Criminal Sociology. ENRICO FERRI, of Turin. (Turin, 1881. Criminology series; London, F. Unwin, 1895. Tr. by J. L. Kelly and J. Lisle. Modern Criminal Science Series; Boston, Little, 1917; London, Heinemann, 1917).

La Criminalita in Relazione col clima. G. ORANO. (Rome, 1882).

La Criminalité Comparée. GABRIEL TARDE. (Paris, Felix Alcan, 1886, 1898, 1902).

La Dinamica del delitto. BATTAGLIA. (Naples, 1886).

Le Crime : Étude Sociale. H. JOLY. (Paris, 1888).

Alcoholisme et Criminalité. J. P. GALLAVARDIN. (Paris, 1889).

La Criminalité en France. A. BERARD. (Grenoble, 1890).

Political Crime [assassination, anarchy, etc.]. LOUIS PROAL. (Paris, Felix Alcan, 1895. Trans. Criminology Series, No. IV.; F. Unwin, 1898).

Théories de la Criminalité. J. DALLEMAGNE. (Paris, 1896).

Le Crime et l'école. J. BONZON. (Paris, 1896).

La lutte contre la criminalité dans les temps modernes. A. DELVINCOURT. (Paris, 1897).

Las Neuvas Teorias de la Criminalitad. [Modern Theories of Criminality]. C. BERNALDO DE QUIROS. (Madrid, 1898. Tr. by Dr. Alphonse de Salvio. Modern Criminal Science Series; Boston, Little, 1911; Heinemann, 1911).

Police et Criminalité : impressions d'un vieux policier. D. R. HAMON. (Paris, 1900).

Le Crime et le suicide passionels. L. PROAL. (Paris, 1900).

La Delinquenza in vari Stati di Europa. AUGUSTE BOSCO. (Rome, 1903).

Das Verbrechen und seine Bekämpfung. [Crime and its Repression]. GUSTAV ASCHAFFENBURG. (Heidelberg, Theime, 1903. Tr. by A. Albrecht. Modern Criminal Science Series; Boston, Little, 1913; Heinemann, 1913).

Criminality and Economic Conditions. W. A. BONGER. (Amsterdam, 1905. Tr. by Henry P. Horton; Heinemann, 1917).

La lutte contre la criminalité en Hongrie. B. KUN and E. LADAY. (Budapest, 1905).

Die Verbrechensbewegung im Ostlichen Europen. (1) Die Kriminalität der Balkanlander. (2) De Kriminalität Russlands. Dr. ARNOLD WADLER. (München, Hans Sachs-Verlag, 1908).

La responsibilité des Criminels. J. GRASSET. (Paris, 1908).

Litterature et Criminalité. SIGHELE. (Paris, Giard & Brière, 1908).

La Criminalité dans l'Ádolescence. G. L. DUPRAT. (Paris, F. Alcan, 1909).

Le Crime et la Société. J. MAXWELL. (Paris, 1909, 1920).

La lutte contre le crime. J. L. DE LANESSAN. (Paris, 1910).

Crime : its causes and remedies. CESARE LOMBROSO. (Tr. Henry P. Horton ; Modern Criminal Science Series ; Boston, Little, 1911 ; Heinemann, 1911).

Le concept social du crime. J. MAXWELL. (Paris, 1914).

Das Verbrechen als Krankheit. Sein Entshehung, Heilung und Verhütung. G. BONNE. (Munich, 1927).

Krieg und Kriminalität in Osterreich. DR. FRANZ EXNER. (Vienna ; Newhaven, U.S.A., Yale University Press, 1927).

Introduzione alla sociologia criminale. F. GRISPIGNI. (Turin, 1928).

Krieg und Kriminalität in Deutschland. M. LIEPMANN. (Stuttgart, 1930).

Kriminalsoziologie : Zugleich eine systematische einführung in die Weiterentwichlung und in die Hilfwissenschaften des Strafrechts. Prof. WILHELM SAUER. (Berlin, 1933).

A III 3 — AMERICA. [*See also* B IV 3 and E III 4].

Increase of Crime and its Cause. MRS. A. B. BOONE. (Boston, 1872).

Cause and Cure of Crime, with a treatise on capital punishment. J. STOLZ. (Philadelphia, Potter, 1880).

Crime : its Nature, Causes, Treatment and Prevention. SANFORD M. GREEN. (Philadelphia, Lippincott, 1889).

Los Causas del Delito. DELLEPIANE. (Buenos Aires, 1892).

Prisoners and Paupers. [Increase of criminals and pauperism in the U.S.A. ; attack on philanthropic institutions]. H. M. BOIES. (New York, Putnam, 1893).

Crime and Criminals. DR. J. S. CHRISTISON. (Chicago, Keener & Co., 1897).

The Relation of Economic Conditions to the Causes of Crime. CARROL D. WRIGHT. (Philadelphia, Amer. Academy Pol. and Social Science, 1900).

Crime in its relation to Social Progress. [Columbia University Studies]. ARTHUR CLEVELAND HALL. (New York, Macmillan, 1902). [Contains bibliography].

Responsibility for Crime : an investigation of the nature and causes of crime and means of prevention. P. A. PARSONS. (New York, Columbia University, 1909 ; Longmans, London).

Criminal responsibility and social restraint. ROY MADDING MCCONNELL. (New York, Scribner, 1912 ; Murray, 1912).

The Present Day Problem of Crime. A. H. CURRIER. (Boston, Gorham Press, 1912).

The Cause and Cure of Crime. CHARLES RICHARDSON HENDERSON, University of Chicago. (Chicago, McClurg & Co., 1914).

Crime Prevention. ARTHUR WOODS, formerly Police Commissioner, New York City. (Oxford University Press, 1919).

Crime : its Causes and Treatment. CLARENCE DARROW, U.S. Counsel. (New York, Crowell, 1922 ; London, Harrap, 1922, 1923 ; Watts, 1934).

Problems of Modern American Crime. VERONICA and PAUL KING. (Heath Cranton, 1926).

Modern Crime : its Prevention and Punishment. CLYDE L. KING. (Annals of the American Academy of Political Science, May, 1926 ; Concord, New Hampshire, 1926).

Crime and the Criminal Law in the United States considered primarily in their present day social aspects. HARRY BEST. (New York, Macmillan Company, 1930). [Has bibliography].

Battling the Crime Wave. Applying sense and science to the repression of Crime. H. E. BARNES. (Boston, U.S.A. ; Stratford, 1931).

Crime. Art. in 'Encyclopaedia of the Social Sciences,' Vol. IV. THORSTEN SELLIN. (Macmillan, 1931). [Has bibliography].

A IV—STUDIES OF THE CRIMINAL IN GENERAL

A IV 1 — GENERAL.

The pauper, the thief and the convict : sketches of some of their homes, haunts and habits. THOMAS ARCHER. (Groombridge, 1865).

Bright Stars on a Dark Thread : being a narrative founded on personal adventures among the criminal classes. A. MARSELL. (London, Langley, 1873).

L'uomo delinquente. [Criminal Man]. CESARE LOMBROSO. (Milan, 1876. Translated ; Putnams, 1911).

A Book about Criminals. MRS. S. MEREDITH. (London, Nisbet, 1881).

Criminals. C. D. SAWIN. (Boston, 1890).

The Criminal. HAVELOCK ELLIS. (Walter Scott, 1889, 1890, 1901, 1907, 1910).

Abnormal Man : Essays in Education and Crime. ARTHUR MACDONALD. (Washington, U.S.A., Govt. Printing Press, 1893).

The Criminal : his personnel and environment : a scientific study. REV. AUGUST. DRÄHMS, Chaplain to St. Quentin Prison, California. (New York ; Macmillan, 1900). [Contains list of works on criminology].

The Study of the Criminal. JAMES DEVON. (Glasgow, 1902).

Experimental Sociology. Descriptive and analytical. Delinquents. FRANCES A. KELLOR. (Macmillan, 1902). [A study of negro women prisoners in the Southern States].

The Criminal Classes : causes and cures. D. R. MILLER. (Dayton, 1903).

Les Criminels. C. PERRIER. (Paris, 1905).

Criminals and Crime : Some Facts and Suggestions. SIR ROBERT ANDERSON. (Nisbet, 1907).

The Indian Criminal. H. L. ADAM. (John Milne, 1909).

Courts, Criminals and the Camorra. ARTHUR TRAIN, formerly Asst. District Attorney, New York County. (Chapman & Hall, 1912).

The Criminal and the Community. JAMES DEVON, Medical Officer, H.M. Prison, Glasgow. (John Lane, 1912, 1913).

How Criminals are made and prevented : a retrospect of forty years. CANON J. W. HORSLEY. (F. Unwin, 1913).

The English Convict. DR. CHARLES GORING. (Wyman, 1913).

The Individual Delinquent : a text book of diagnosis and prognosis for all concerned in understanding offenders. WILLIAM HEALY, M.D. (Heinemann, 1915).

Sidelights in Criminal Matters. J. C. GOODWIN. (Hutchinson, 1923).

The Criminal as a Human Being. G. S. DOUGHERTY. (New York, Appleton, 1924).

The Criminal [professional criminals]. SIR BASIL THOMSON. (Hodder & Stoughton, 1922, 1925).

The Soul of a Criminal. J. C. GOODWIN. (Hutchinson, 1924).

The Underworld : a series of adventures and reminiscences in many lands. H. ASHTON-WOLFE. (Hurst & Blackett, 1926).

The Community and the Criminal. A guide to Catholic Service. FRANCIS DAY. (Oxford Catholic Social Guild, 1926).

The Child of Circumstance [deals with the criminal from a scientific point of view]. DR. ALBERT WILSON. (Bale, Sons & Danielsson, 1928).

The Criminal. A Study. H. A. GEISERT. (St. Louis, Mo., 1930).

Prisoner at the Bar. ARTHUR GARDNER [Prison Visitor]. (P. Allan, 1931).

Genius and the Criminal. HENRY T. F. RHODES. (Murray, 1932).

The Lawbreaker. E. ROY CALVERT and MRS. THEODORA CALVERT. (Routledge, 1933). [Represents an unofficial and reformist standpoint: a critical study of the modern treatment of crime].

Crime; London's Underworld: a month's sojourn in the crime centres of the Metropolis. SYDNEY HORLER. (Hutchinson, 1934).

A IV 2—CRIMINAL ANTHROPOLOGY.

L'uomo delinquente. CESARE LOMBROSO [1836–1909]. (Milan, 1876. Translation in 'Criminal Man,' according to Lombroso's classification summarised by his daughter Gina Lombroso Ferrero; Putnam, 1911; contains list of chief works).

Le Criminel et l'anthropologia Criminelle. F. J. SAINTE AUBIN. (Grenoble, 1889).

Criminal anthropology. HAMILTON D. WEY. (New York, Elmira, 1890).

Les Habitués des Prisons de Paris: Etude d'anthropologie. DR. EMILE LAURENT. (Paris, Masson, 1890).

L'anthropologie Criminelle. X. FRANCOTTE. (Paris, 1891).

The New School of Criminal Anthropology. G. J. FLETCHER. (Washington, 1891).

Der Verbrecher in anthropologischer Beziehung. DR. A. BAER. (Leipzig, 1893).

L'omidicio nell'antropologia Criminale. ENRICO FERRI. (Turin, 1895).

La Antropologia Criminale. B. W. ANDRADE. (Madrid, 1896).

The Criminal. HAVELOCK ELLIS. (Walter Scott, 1901). [Criminal anthropology in England, Continent and America].

Handleiding bij de Studie der Crimineele anthropologie. A. ALETRINO. (Amsterdam, 1904).

Antropologia Criminale. S. FRESCHI. (Milan, 1905).

The Principles of Anthropology and Sociology in their relation to Criminal Procedure. MAURICE PARMELEE. (Macmillan, 1908).

Antropologia Criminal. F. CARPENA. (Madrid, 1909).

Schedules of Measurement and General Anthropological Data; supplement to 'The English Convict: a Statistical Study.' DR. CHARLES GORING. (Wyman, 1913).

Estudios sobre antropologia criminal en las Islas Filipinas. S. DE LOS ANGELES. (Manila, 1919).

The Child of Circumstance. DR. ALBERT WILSON. (Bale, Sons & Danielsson, London, 1928).

Crime as Destiny: a study of Criminal Twins. PROF. DR. JOHANNES LANGE. Tr. by Charlotte Haldane. (Allen & Unwin, 1931).

Constitution—Types in Delinquency. WILHELMUS A. WILLEMSE. (Kegan Paul, 1932).

A IV 3 — CRIMINAL STATISTICS.

History and Organization of Criminal Statistics in the United States. L. N. ROBINSON. (Boston; Houghton, Mifflin, 1911).

The English Convict: A Statistical Study. DR. CHARLES GORING, H.M. Prison, Parkhurst. (London, Wyman, 1913).

Criminal Statistics, England and Wales. Home Office. (H.M.S.O. ; annual).

Criminal Statistics, Scotland. (H.M.S.O. ; annual).

Survey of Criminal Statistics in the United States for the National Commission on Law Observance and Enforcement. S. B. WARNER. (Washington, 1929).

Uniform Crime Reports for the United States and its Possessions. (Published monthly, up to 1930, by the Committee on Uniform Crime Records, 261, Broadway, New York City ; and continued by the Bureau of Investigation, Dept. of Justice, United States ; 1930—).

Crime and Criminal Statistics in Boston. S. B. WARNER. (Harvard University Press ; London, H. Milford, 1934).

A IV 4 — CRIMINAL LANGUAGE.

Slang Dictionary of New York, London and Paris. A collection of strange figures of speech, expressive terms and odd phrases used in the leading cities of the World. Their origin, meaning and application. (New York, National Police Gazette, official, 1890).

A V—JUVENILE DELINQUENCY. [*See also* F VII 3, H I, H II, & H III].

Report on the Committee for investigating the causes of the Alarming Increase of Juvenile Delinquency in the Metropolis. (London, 1816).

Juvenile Offenders. Remarks on the cause and state of Juvenile Crime in the Metropolis, with hints for preventing its increase. W. BUCHANAN. (London, 1846, 1847).

Extent and Causes of Juvenile Depravity. THOMAS BEGGS. (London, C. Gilpin, 1849).

Juvenile Delinquents : their condition and treatment. MARY CARPENTER. (London, Cash, 1853).

Juvenile Crime : its causes, character and cure. S. P. DAY. (London, Hope, 1858).

Half Century with Juvenile Delinquents. B. K. PIERCE. (New York, 1869).

The Gaol Cradle : who rocks it ? [Juvenile crime, unemployment and pauperism]. B. WAUGH. (London, Strahan, 1873).

Physical Training of Youthful Criminals. H. D. WEY. (Boston, 1888).

Le Criminel Type dans Quelques Formes Graves de la Criminalité [concerning juvenile criminality]. DR. ARTHUR MACDONALD. (Paris, 1894).

Youthful eccentricity a precursor of Crime. F. E. WINSLOW. (New York, Funk, 1895).

Juvenile Offenders. REV. W. D. MORRISON [H.M. Prison, Wandsworth]. (Criminology Series ; F. Unwin, 1896, 1897 ; New York, Appleton, 1897).

The Making of the Criminal [deals with juvenile crime]. C. E. B. RUSSELL and L. M. RIGBY. (Macmillan, 1906).

Treatment of Juvenile Delinquents. R. R. PERKINS. (Rockford, 1906).

La Criminalité infantile. E. LAURENT. (Paris, A. Maloine, 1906).

Child Problems. G. B. MANGOLD. (Macmillan, 1907, 1910).

The Young Malefactor—a Study in juvenile delinquency, its causes and treatment. THOMAS TRAVIS. (New York, Crowell, 1908, 1912). [Contains bibliography].

Juvenile Crime and Reformation, including stigmata of degeneration. ARTHUR MACDONALD. (Washington, U.S.A. ; Govt. Printing Office, 1908). [Contains bibliography].

Young Gaol Birds. CHARLES E. B. RUSSELL, Hon. Sec. Lads' Club, Manchester. (Macmillan, 1910, 1919).

The Junior Republic. W. R. GEORGE. (New York, Appleton, 1910).

Delinquent Child and the Home. S. P. BRECKINRIDGE and E. ABBOTT. (New York; Charities Publishing Committee, 1912).

Across the Bridges. ALEXANDER PATERSON. (E. Arnold, 1912).

American Bad Boys in the Making. ALEXANDER H. STEWART. (New York, Lechner, 1912).

Citizens Made and Unmade. W. R. GEORGE and L. R. STOWE. (Cambridge, U.S.A.; Riverside Press, 1912).

Young Delinquents. [A study of reformatory and industrial schools]. MARY S. BARNETT. (Methuen, 1913).

Justice and the Child. DOUGLAS POPLAR. (Constable, 1915).

The State and the Child. W. CLARKE HALL. (Swarthmore Press, 1917).

Romance of Child Reformation. M. [later, SIR MEYER] SPIELMAN. (Reformatory and Refuge Union, 1920). [Deals with the neglected and delinquent child].

Juvenile Delinquency. HENRY H. GODDARD. (Kegan Paul, 1922).

The Unadjusted Girl, with cases and standpoint for behaviour analysis. W. J. THOMAS. (Boston, U.S.A., Little, 1923; Criminal Science Monograph, No. IV.); Routledge, Kegan Paul, 1923, 1924).

The Young Delinquent. CYRIL BURT. (University of London Press, 1925).

The Child, the Clinic and the Court. JAMES ADAMS. (New York, 1925).

Youth in Conflict. MIRIAM VAN WATERS. (Methuen, 1926).

The delinquent boy: a socio-psychological study. JOHN SLAWSON. (Boston, Badgers, 1926).

The problem child in School. MARY B. SAYLES. (New York: Joint Committee on Methods of Preventing Juvenile Delinquency, 1926).

Report from the Departmental Committee on Juvenile Delinquency. [Appointed in 1925 by the Home Office]. Cmd. 2831. (H.M.S.O., 1927).

Report of the Departmental Committee on the Treatment of young offenders, etc. [Scotland]. (H.M.S.O., 1928).

Autolycus [deals with the youthful delinquent]. R. G. GORDON. (Kegan Paul, 1928).

Delinquents and Criminals, their making and unmaking [work of juvenile courts in Chicago and Boston]. DR. W. HEALY and DR. A. F. BRONNER. (New York, Macmillan, 1928).

Boys in Trouble [a study of adolescent crime and its treatment]. MRS. L. LE MESURIER, leader of the women workers at the Boys' Prison, London. (Murray, 1931).

London's Bad Boys. S. F. HATTON. (Chapman & Hall, 1931).

The Children and Young Persons Act, 1933. Ed. HON. DOUGALL MESTON. (Sweet & Maxwell, 1933).

The Law relating to Children and Young Persons. SIR W. CLARKE HALL and A. C. L. MORRISON. (Butterworth, 1933).

One thousand Juvenile Delinquents: their treatment by Court and clinic. SHELDON GLUECK and ELEANOR GLUECK. (Harvard Univ. Press; Oxford Univ. Press, 1934).

Classified List of Child-saving Institutions in Great Britain and Ireland [more than 1300]. Reformatory and Refuge Union. (London; 26th Edn., 1935).

A VI—FEMALE CRIME

The Female Offender [La Donna Delinquente]. CESARE LOMBROSO and WILLIAM FERRERO. (Turin, 1895). English Translation ed. by W. Douglas Morrison. (The Criminology Series; Unwin, 1895). [Study of physical characteristics of female criminals by Italian criminologists].

Femmes Criminelles. G. MACÉ. (Paris, 1904).

La femme Criminelle. C. GRANIER. (Paris, 1906).

Woman and Crime. H. L. ADAM. (Werner Laurie, 1912, 1914).

A Study of Women Delinquents in New York State. MABEL RUTH FERNALD. (Publications of Bureau of Social Hygiene; New York, Century Co., 1920).

Crook Janes. A study of the woman criminal. NETLEY LUCAS. (Stanley Paul, 1926).

Feminine Frailty [Laura Bell, Edith Carew, etc.]. H. WYNDHAM. (Benn, 1929).

Annals of Crime: the story of Eleven extraordinary Women. [Mrs. Maybrick, etc.]. W. H. WILLIAMSON. (Routledge, 1930).

Women and Crime. CECIL BISHOP, C.I.D., and BASIL FRANCIS. (Chatto & Windus, 1931).

Women of the Underworld. MRS. CECIL CHESTERTON. (Stanley Paul, 1931).

Queens of Crime. [Mary Bateman, Marquise de Brinvilliers, Elizabeth Brownrigg, Gesina Gottfried, etc.]. LEONARD R. GRIBBLE. (Hurst & Blackett, 1932).

Such Women are Dangerous. [30 studies of women criminals: Amy Dugan, etc.]. DR. HAROLD DEARDEN. (Hutchinson, 1933).

Studies in the Psychology of Delinquency. [Case Studies of 200 girls and women for the Medical Research Council]. DR. GRACE PAILTHORPE. (H.M.S.O., 1933).

Five Hundred Delinquent Women. S. GLUECK and E. GLUECK. (New York, Knopf, 1934).

She stands Accused [female crime]. VICTOR MACCLURE. (Harrap, 1935).

A VII—PSYCHOLOGY OF CRIME

A VII 1 — GENERAL. [*See* A VII 2 for Insanity].

Abnormal Man, being essays on education and crime and related subjects. A. MACDONALD. (Washington, U.S.A.; Govt. Printing Press, 1893. [Contains large bibliography].

Moral Pathology. A. E. GILES. (London, Sonnenschein, 1895).

The criminal mind [L'ame de criminel]. From the French of DR. MAURICE DE FLEURY. (Paris, 1898; London, Downey, 1901).

The universal illusion of free will and criminal responsibility. A. F. HAMON. (London, University Press, 1899).

La Psychologie Criminelle. P. KOVALEVSKY. (Paris, 1903).

Kriminal Psychologie und Strafrechtliche Psychopathologie auf Naturwissenschaftlicher Grundlage. R. SOMNER. (Leipzig, 1904).

Criminal Responsibility. DR. CHARLES MERCIER. (Clarendon Press, 1905).

Education, Personality and Crime. DR. A. WILSON. (Greening, 1908).

On the Witness Stand: Essays on Psychology of Crime. HUGO MÜNSTERBERG, Prof. Harvard University. (New York; Doubleday, Page, 1909; Clark Boardman, 1923).

Unfinished Man: a Scientific analysis of the Psychopath or Human Degenerate. DR. A. WILSON. (Greening, 1910).

Criminal Psychology. A Manual for Judges, Practitioners and Students. HANS GROSS, Professor of Criminal Law, University of Gratz, Austria. Tr. by Dr. Horace M. Kallen. (Modern Criminal Science Series; Boston, U.S.A., Little, 1911; Heinemann, 1911).

Psychology and Crime. T. HOLMES. (Dent, 1912).

Criminal Responsibility and Social Restraint. R. M. McCONNELL. (Murray, 1912).

Pathological Lying, Accusation and Swindling: a study in forensic psychology. DR. WILLIAM HEALY. (Criminal Science Monograph, No. 1; Heinemann, 1915).

Studies in Forensic Psychiatry. B. GLUECK. (Heinemann, 1916).

Mental Conflicts and Misconduct. DR. W. HEALY. (Boston, Little, 1917; Kegan Paul, 1919).

The Psychology of the Criminal, with special reference to psycho-analysis. MAURICE HAMBLIN SMITH, Medical officer of H.M. Prison, Birmingham. (Methuen, 1922).

Psychology of Misconduct, Vice and Crime. BERNARD HOLLANDER. (George Allen, 1922).

Crime, Abnormal Minds and the Law. ERNEST B. HOAG and E. H. WILLIAMS. (Indianopolis, U.S.A.; Bobbs-Merrill Co., 1923).

Mental Disorder and the Criminal Law. S. S. GLUECK. (Boston; Little, Brown, 1925).

The Soul of a Criminal. JOHN C. GOODWIN. (Hutchinson, 1925).

Criminal Intelligence. CARL MURCHISON. (Intern. Univ. Series in Psychology, etc.; Clark University, Worcester, Mass., U.S.A., 1926).

Psychotechnik und Polizei: Probleme, Methoden und Erfahrungen. R. W. SCHULTE. (Oldenburg, 1926).

Punishment and Personality. [Visits to prisons; the criminal mind; conversations with doctors and chaplains]. HAROLD BEGBIE. (Mills & Boon, 1927).

An Introduction to Forensic Psychiatry in the Criminal Court. DR. W. NORWOOD EAST. (Churchill, 1927).

The Psychology of Murder: a study in Criminal Psychology. ANDREAS BJERRE. Tr. from Swedish by E. Classen. (Longmans, 1927).

Emotion and Delinquency [study of 500 cases]. DR. L. GRIMBERG. (Library of Educational Psychology; Routledge, Kegan Paul, 1928).

The Relation of the Skull and Brain to Crime. DR. W. NORWOOD EAST. (Henderson Trust Lectures; Edinburgh, Oliver & Boyd, 1928).

Crime and the Man [analysis of the criminal mind]. ELLIS ROBERTS. (Arrowsmith, 1930).

Psychic Self Defence. A study of occult pathology and criminality. DION FORTUNE. (Rider, 1930).

The Mind of the Murderer. DR. HAROLD DEARDEN. (G. Bles, 1930).

The Personality of Criminals. ALBERT W. STEARNS. (Boston, U.S.A.; Beacon Press, 1931).

The Criminal, the Judge, and the Public: a Psychological Analysis. DR. FRANZ ALEXANDER and H. STAUB. Tr. by Gregory Zilboorg. (Allen & Unwin, 1931).

Genius and Criminal: a Study in Rebellion. H. T. F. RHODES. (Murray, 1932).

Studies in the Psychology of Delinquency. DR. GRACE W. PAILTHORPE. (Medical Research Council, 1932).

Crime, Law and Social Science. J. MICHAEL and MORTIMER J. ADLER. (International Library of Psychology; Kegan Paul, 1933).

Prisoner at the Bar. Story Studies of the Criminal Mind. ANTHONY L. ELLIS. (Heath Cranton, 1934).

A VII 2 — INSANITY.

Observations on the Criminal Responsibility of the Insane, founded on the trials of J. Hill and W. Dove. CALEB WILLIAMS. (London, Churchill, 1856).

Madness and Crime. CLARK BELL. (New York, 1884).

Criminal Responsibility of the Insane. [Lecture]. C. J. CULLINGWORTH. (Manchester, J. E. Cornish, 1885).

Insanity of Passion and Crime. DR. L. S. FORBES WINSLOW. (London, John Ouseley, 1898).

Insanity in India: with reference to the relation of Crime and insanity. G. F. W. EWENS. (Calcutta; Thacker, Spink, 1908).

Recollections of Forty Years [account of some famous criminal lunacy cases, English and American]. DR. L. S. FORBES WINSLOW. (John Ouseley, 1910).

Crimes and Insanity. DR. CHARLES MERCIER. (Williams & Norgate, 1911; New York, Holt, 1911).

Psychology of Insanity. BERNARD HART. (Cambridge Univ. Press, 1912; 4th edn., 1928).

The Criminal Imbecile: an analysis of three remarkable murder cases. HENRY H. GODDARD. (New York, Macmillan, 1915).

The Defective Delinquent and the Insane. HENRY A. COTTON. (Princetown, U.S.A.; Louis Clark Vanuxem Lectures, 1921).

Insanity and Mental Deficiency in relation to Legal Responsibility. WILLIAM G. H. COOK. (Routledge, 1921).

Insanity and the Criminal Law. WILLIAM A. WHITE. (New York, Macmillan, 1923).

Insanity and the Criminal. JOHN C. GOODWIN. (New York, Macmillan; Hutchinson, 1923).

Insanity and Crime. Report of Committee on Insanity Plea. (H.M.S.O.; Cmd. 2005; 1923).

Crime and Insanity. DR. W. C. SULLIVAN, Med. Supt., Broadmoor Criminal Lunatic Asylum. (E. Arnold, 1924).

Mental Disorders and the Criminal Law. S. S. GLUECK. (Boston, U.S.A.; Little, Brown, 1925).

Crime and Insanity. BARON DARLING. (J. A. Allen, 1925).

'Guilty but Insane,' a Broadmoor Autobiography. 'WARMARK.' (Chapman & Hall, 1931). [Account of the criminal lunatic asylum].

A VIII—RECIDIVISM

La Recidive. L. ANDRE. (Paris, 1892).

Recividism. Habitual Criminality and Habitual Petty Delinquency. A problem of Sociology. DR. J. F. SUTHERLAND. (Edinburgh, Green, 1908).

The Problem of the recidivist. ELTON J. MORRISON. (Madison, U.S.A.; Univ. of Wisconsin, 1916).

The Problem of the Old Offender. C. M. KNOWLES. (*Police Journal,* Vol. IV., p. 506, Oct., 1931).

Report from the Department Committee on Methods of dealing with persistent offenders. Cmd. 4090. (H.M.S.O.; 1932).

B. CRIMINALS AND CRIMINAL CASES

B I—COLLECTIONS OF CASES

B I 1—CRIMINALS.

The Belman of London : Bringing to Light the most notorious villanies that are now practised in the Kingdom. THOMAS DEKKER. (London, 1608. The Temple Classics, Dent, 1896). [*See also* 'The Elizabethan Underworld,' *infra*].

History of the Lives and Actions of the most famous Highwaymen, Street Robbers, etc. CAPT. CHARLES JOHNSON. (Edinburgh, Thomson, 1813 ; also Longman ; also Willoughby, 1839).

Lives and Exploits of Banditti and Robbers in all Parts of the World. CHARLES MACFARLANE. 2 vols. (London, Bull, 1833).

Lives of Twelve Bad Men ; *Original studies of Eminent Scoundrels* [McLaine ; Fighting Fitzgerald ; Edward Kelly, Bushranger, etc.]. T. SECCOMBE. (Unwin, 1894, 1895, 1899).

Criminals I have known. MAJOR A. GRIFFITHS. (Chapman & Hall, 1895).

A Book of Scoundrels. CHAS. WHIBLEY. (Heinemann, 1897).

Lives of Twelve Bad Women. A. VINCENT. (Unwin, 1898).

Some Distinguished Victims of the Scaffold. HORACE BLEACKLEY. (Kegan Paul, 1905).

Known to the Police. THOS. HOLMES, Secretary to the Howard Association. (Arnold, 1908 ; Nelson, 1915).

Scarlet Sinners. Stories of Notorious Criminals and Crimes. D. DONOVAN [*i.e.*, J. E. MUDDOCK]. (Newnes, 1910).

London's Underworld. T. HOLMES. (Dent, 1912).

Walter Greenway, Spy, and others, sometime criminal. R. HOLMES, Pclice Court Missionary. (Blackwood, 1916).

A Book of Remarkable Criminals [Charles Peace, Robert Butler, Dernes Castaing, Prof. Webster, etc.]. H. B. IRVING. (Cassell, 1918).

Remarkable Rogues : the careers of some noted Criminals of Europe and America. [Marie Tarnowska, Jeanne Daniloff, G. Gottfried, Belle Star, Anna Schnieder, etc.]. C. KINGSTON. (John Lane, 1921).

Queer People. SIR BASIL THOMSON. (Hodder & Stoughton, 1922).

The Sidelights of London. J. A. R. CAIRNS. (Hutchinson, 1923).

The Underworld of London. S. T. FELSTEAD. (Murray, 1923).

Rogues and Scoundrels. P. W. SERGEANT. (Hutchinson, 1924).

Keys to Crookdom [analysis of every type of criminal]. G. C. HENDERSON. (New York, Appleton, 1924, 1925).

A Gallery of Rogues. [Crime and clairvoyance, Peace, Corder, Dr. Pritchard, etc.]. C. KINGSTON. (Stanley Paul, 1924).

The Fair Countess and [7] *other Studies* [historical]. W. ROUGHEAD. (Edinburgh, Green, 1924).

Queer Fish. J. C. GOODWIN. (Hutchinson, 1925).

Criminal Yarns. T. C. BRIDGES. (Hutchinson, 1925).

Crooks ; *Confessions, etc.* NETLEY LUCAS. (Hurst & Blackett, 1925, 1926).

London and its Criminals. NETLEY LUCAS. (Williams & Norgate, 1926).

Crook Janes. NETLEY LUCAS. (Stanley Paul, 1926).

Lives of the most remarkable Criminals who have been condemned and executed for Murder; the Highway, Housebreaking, Street Robberies, Coining and other offences [Jack Sheppard, Jonathan Wild, etc.]. (Originally published, 1735; new edition, ed. ARTHUR L. HAYWARD. Routledge, 1927).

Crook Pie. J. C. GOODWIN. (Alston Rivers, 1927).

Outlaws of Modern Days. H. ASHTON-WOLFE. (Cassell, 1927).

Enemies of Society. CHARLES KINGSTON. (Stanley Paul, 1927).

Twelve Monstrous Criminals [Nero to Rasputin]. P. B. BARRY. (Hutchinson, 1927).

The Underworld. H. ASHTON-WOLFE. (Hurst & Blackett, 1927).

Crooks and Crime: the Methods of Criminals and their circumvention. J. KENNETH FERRIER. (Seeley, Service, 1928).

Rogues and Adventurers. CHARLES KINGSTON. (Lane, 1928).

Masters of Crime: Studies of Multiple Murders. GUY B. H. LOGAN. (Stanley Paul, 1928).

Crooks of the Underworld. CHARLES G. GORDON. (G. Bles, 1929).

Sinners down the Centuries [69 B.C. to A.D. 1886]. P. B. BARRY. (Jarrolds, 1929).

Bad Companions: Lives of Criminals. W. ROUGHEAD. (Edinburgh, Green, 1930).

International Criminals: Past and Present. FREDERIC BOUTET. (Hutchinson, 1930).

Lawbreakers. CHARLES KINGSTON. (John Lane, 1930).

Five Hundred Criminal Careers. SHELDON GLUECK and ELEANOR T. GLUECK. (Knopf, 1930).

Strange Company. S. THEODORE FELSTEAD. (Hutchinson, 1930).

The Elizabethan Underworld. [Works of Harman, Middleton, Greene and Dekker]. A. V. JUDGES. (Routledge, 1930).

Picturesque Rogues. ROBERT L. HADFIELD. (H. F. & G. Witherby, 1931).

Women Bluebeards, etc. ELLIOTT O'DONNELL. (Stanley Paul, 1931).

All the Sinners. HERBERT ARTHUR. (John Long, 1931).

The Art of the Criminal. ARTHUR R. G. GARDNER. (Philip Allan, 1931).

Genius and Criminal: Study in Rebellion. HENRY T. F. RHODES. (Murray, 1932).

Twenty Human Monsters in Purple and Rags, from Caligula to Landru, A.D. 12 to A.D. 1922. P. B. BARRY. (Jarrolds, 1932).

In Queer Street [studies of Scottish criminals]. W. ROUGHEAD. (Edinburgh, Green, 1932).

A History of the lives and actions of the most notorious highwaymen, footpads, etc. CAPT. ALEX. SMITH. Ed. A. L. Hayward. (Routledge, 1933).

The Newgate Calendar or the Malefactor's Bloody Register [Monson and others]. Ed. B. Laurie. (New edition, 2 vols.; T. Werner Laurie, 1933).

Rogues Walk Here [9 cases]. W. ROUGHEAD. (Cassell, 1934).

Rogues March [14 cases, including those of the Stauntons, Redpath, Adam Worth, etc.]. G. DILNOT. (G. Bles, 1934).

B I 2 — CRIMES.

[Many collections were published in the 18th and early in the 19th Century : a selection has been made].

The Terrific Register, or a Record of Crimes, etc. (London, Sherwood Jones, 1825).

The New and Complete Newgate Calendar. WILLIAM JACKSON. 5 vols. (London, Alex. Hogg, 1828).

Annals of Crime : a New Newgate Calendar. 2 vols. (London, W. C. Clark, 1837).

The Chronicles of Crime, or the new Newgate Calendar ; being a series of Memoirs and anecdotes of Notorious Characters . . . to 1841. 2 vols. CAMDEN PELHAM. (London, Miles, 1841, 1886, 1891).

The Complete Newgate Calendar. [CAPT. CHAS. JOHNSON, 1734 ; CAPT. ALEX. SMITH, 1792 ; Histories of the Lives and Adventures of various Highwaymen, Murderers, Pirates, etc., 1719. The Tyburn Chronicle, 1768. The Malefactor's Register, 1796. GEO. BORROW'S Celebrated Trials, 1825. The Newgate Calendar, by A. KNAPP and W. BALDWIN, 1824. CAMDEN PELHAM'S Chronicles of Crime, 1841]. Ed. by J. L. Rayner and G. T. Crook ; 5 vols. (Navarre Society, 1926).

Strange Crimes. WILLIAM WESTALL. (Ward & Downey, 1890).

Studies in Black and Red [30 tales of notable crimes : Arnold du Tilb, Charles Peace, Madeline Smith, J. B. Rush, David Haggart, etc.]. JOS. FORSTER. (Ward & Downey, 1896).

Mysteries of Police and Crime. MAJOR A. GRIFFITHS. (2 vols.; Cassell, 1898, 1903. Special edition, 3 vols., 1920).

The Byeways of Crime : with some stories from the Black Museum. R. T. POWER-BERREY. (London, Greening, 1899).

Masterpieces of Crime. A. D. VANDAM. (Routledge, 1905).

A Great Conspiracy. [The Fenian Movement]. SIR ROBERT ANDERSON. (Murray, 1909).

Survivors' Tales of Sixteen Famous Crimes. [Moat Farm murder, etc.]. Ed. Walter Wood. (Cassell, 1916).

Crimes of Old London. MARJORIE BOWAN [pseud., *i.e.*, GABRIELLE M. VERE LONG]. (Odhams, 1919).

Famous Crimes and Criminals. [38 Cases : Gold-dust Teddy, Chicago May, Mignon, Jim the Penman, etc.]. C. McCLUER STEVENS. (Stanley Paul, 1924).

Celebrated Crimes. GEORGE DILNOT. (Stanley Paul, 1925).

Black Fame : Stories of Crime and Criminals. [Peace, Crippin, Whittaker Wright, etc.]. J. C. ELLIS. (Hutchinson, 1926).

Under the Black Flag. DON L. SEITZ. (The Rogues Gallery ; Stanley Paul, 1927).

World Famous Crimes. F. A. MACKENZIE. (G. Bles, 1927).

Forgotten Crimes. J. W. POYNTER. (Selwyn & Blount, 1928).

Warped in the Making : Crimes of Hate and Love. H. ASHTON-WOLFE. (Hurst & Blackett, 1928).

Crime on the Continent. HORACE WYNDHAM. (T. Butterworth, 1928).

Look upon the Prisoner. Studies in Crime. A. H. M. BRICE (late Recorder of Tewkesbury). Ed. by Alexander Cairns. (Hutchinson, 1928).

Guilty or Not Guilty : Stories of Celebrated Crimes. [Mary Ashford, Bill o'Jack, Browne and Kennedy. Voirbo, Maynard]. GUY B. H. LOGAN. (Stanley Paul, 1928 ; Rich & Cowan, 1933).

The Thrill of Evil: Queer and Fantastic Crimes. H. ASHTON-WOLFE. (Hurst & Blackett, 1928).

Malice Domestic. Accounts of Celebrated Crimes. W. ROUGHEAD. (Edinburgh, Green, 1928).

Feminine Frailty. HORACE WYNDHAM. (Benn, 1929).

A Book of Crimes. [12 studies of 17th and 19th centuries]. A. SALUSBURY MCNALTY. (Elkin, Matthews & Marrot, 1929).

Extraordinary Crimes. [18 cases]. JOHN LAURENCE. (Sampson Low, 1929).

The Secret History of Great Crimes. W. H. STEER. (London; A. H. Stockwell, 1929).

The Bench and the Dock. [Crime, criminals and detection]. C. KINGSTON. (Stanley Paul, 1930).

Dramas of the Dock. True Stories of Crime. GUY B. H. LOGAN. (Stanley Paul, 1930).

True Stories of Immortal Crimes. [Continent and America]. H. ASHTON-WOLFE. (Hurst & Blackett, 1930).

International Crimes, Past and Present. F. BOUTET. (Hutchinson, 1930).

More Stories of Immortal Crimes. H. ASHTON-WOLFE. (Hurst & Blackett, 1931).

Guilty or Not Guilty? [50 cases from many countries]. GUY RUSSELL. (Hutchinson 1931).

Seaside Crimes. J. LAURENCE. (Sampson Low, 1931).

Further Tales of Immortal Crimes. H. ASHTON-WOLFE. (Hurst & Blackett, 1931).

The Best Laid Schemes. [Studies in Crime]. H. W. TWYMAN. (London; Harold Shaylor, 1931).

The Criminal Annual, 1931. Ed. Robert Curzon. (F. V. White & Co., 1932).

Strange Crimes. H. ASHTON-WOLFE. (Hurst & Blackett, 1932).

Crimes of the Year. JOSEPH GOLLOMB. (Allen & Unwin, 1932).

Crimes and Cases of 1933. ROLAND WILD. (Rich & Cowan, 1934).

True Crime. [Omnibus of books by J. C. GOODWIN, P. B. BARRY and DR. RAPPEPORT]. (Rich & Cowan, 1934).

Trunk Crimes, Past and Present. LEONARD LEWIS. (Hutchinson, 1934).

Crimes and Cases of 1934. ROLAND WILD. (Rich & Cowan, 1935).

Continental Crimes. E. L. VON SONNENBERG and O. TRETTIN. (G. Bles, 1935).

B I 3—SOME MYSTERIES.

The Penge Mystery: the story of the Stauntons. H. L. ADAM. (Pearson, 1913). *See also* under F II 1.

The Bravo Mystery [1876] *and other Cases.* SIR JOHN HALL. (Lane, 1923).

Unsolved Murder Mysteries. C. PEARCE. (Stanley Paul, 1924).

The Overbury Mystery. A Chronicle of Fact and Drama of the Law. Judge E. A. [later SIR EDWARD] PARRY. (Fisher, Unwin, 1925).

Strange Disappearances. ELLIOTT O'DONNELL. (Lane, 1927.)

Riddles of Crimes. Fourteen Murder Mysteries that were never solved. ELIZABETH VILLIERS. (Werner Laurie, 1928).

Ten Real Murder Mysteries. [American]. SIDNEY SUTHERLAND. (Putnam, 1929).

Great Thames Mysteries. ELLIOTT O'DONNELL. (Selwyn & Blount, 1930).

B II—STUDIES OF INDIVIDUAL CRIMINALS AND CASES

B II 1 — CASE HISTORIES.

The History of Burke and Hare and of the Resurrectionist Times, a fragment from the Criminal Annals of Scotland. G. MacGregor. (Glasgow, Morrison, 1884).

Deacon Brodie or Behind the Mask. Dick Donovan [*i.e.*, J. E. Muddock]. (Chatto & Windus, 1901).

Jim the Penman : The Life story of one of the most astounding criminals that ever lived [James Townsend Saward]. Dick Donovan [*i.e.* J. E. Muddock]. (Newnes, 1901, 1913, 1917).

The Romantic Career of a Great Criminal : a memoir of Charles Peace. N. Kynaston Gaskell. (London, N. W. Gaskell, 1906). [*See also* B I 1; F II 1; and below].

Pritchard the Poisoner. H. L. Adam. (C. A. Pearson, 1913).

A Master of Crime : the life story of Charles Williams. (Odhams, 1918).

The [Elizabeth] *Canning Wonder.* Arthur Machen. (Chatto & Windus, 1925).

The Life and Career of Dr. William Palmer, of Rugeley. George Fletcher. (F. Unwin, 1925). [*See also* F II 1].

The Crime and Trial of Leopold and Loeb. M. McKernan. (Allen & Unwin, 1925).

Vidocq : a Master of Crime. E. A. B. Hodgetts. (Selwyn & Blount, 1929).

The Mystery of Jack the Ripper. Leonard Matters. (Hutchinson, 1929).

The Great Pearl Robbery of 1913. A Record of Facts. Christmas Humphreys. (Heinemann, 1929).

The Master Criminal: the life story of Charles Peace. (Pearson, 1930).

The Prince of Pickpockets [George Barrington]. R. S. Lambert. (Faber, 1930).

The Green Bicycle Case [1920]. H. R. Wakefield. (P. Allan, 1930).

The Dartmoor Shepherd : Fifty Years in prison [biography of David Davies]. A. Scriven. (Oswestry, John Ainscow, 1931).

The Devil Man [Charles Peace]. Edgar Wallace. (Collins, 1931).

Underworld : biography of Charles Brooks, criminal. Trevor Allen. (Grant Richards, 1931).

Natural History of a Delinquent Career. Clifford R. Shaw and Maurice E. Moore. (Chicago University Press ; Cambridge University Press, 1931).

Spada the Bandit [last of the Corsican bandits]. Ed. Robert Darrell. (Grayson & Grayson, 1935).

B II 2 — PERSONAL MEMOIRS [*See also* in G IV 3].

Memoirs of Jane Cameron, female convict. A Prison Matron [F. W. Robinson]. 2 vols. (Hurst & Blackett, 1864, 1869).

Forging his own Chains : the autobiography of George Bidwell [Bank of England forgery]. (London, H. C. Mott, 1888, 1891).

Langdon W. Moore: his own story of his eventful life [burglar, safe-blower, etc.]. (Boston, 1893).

A Burglar's Life Story in Glasgow, Edinburgh, London, Crimea, etc. D. Fannan. Ed. J. Wallace. (Glasgow, D. Bryce, 1897).

Hooligan nights : being the life and opinions of a young and impenitent criminal recounted by himself. Ed. Clarence Rook. (Richards, 1899).

The Autobiography of a Thief. Ed. Hutchins Hapgood. (New York : Fox, Duffield, 1903 ; London, Putnam, 1904).

Israel Rank: the autobiography of a criminal. ROY HORNIMAN. (Chatto & Windus, 1907).

Nights with an Old Lag. W. J. WINTLE. (John Ouseley, 1911).

The Autobiography of a Crook [from material supplied by Netley Lucas]. R. L. DEARDEN. (F. Unwin, 1925).

You can't Win: the life story of a thief [American criminal]. JACK BLACK. (Macmillan, 1926).

Lockstep and Corridor [autobiography of a criminal]. Ed. Earle E. Eubank. (Cincinnati, Streit, 1927).

Crime: the autobiography of a Crook. EDDIE GUERIN. (Murray, 1928).

Raffles in Real Life. The Confessions of George Smithson, alias 'Gentleman Joe'. (Hutchinson, 1930).

Crime from the Inside: revelations and confessions of Warder, Confidence Trickster, and 'Fence.' Ed. John Gregory [pseud.]. (Long, 1930).

Hell's Kitchen: being the story of London's Underworld as related by the notorious ex-burglar George Ingram to De Witt Mackenzie. (Herbert Jenkins, 1930).

'Guilty but Insane': a Broadmoor autobiography. 'WARMARK.' (Chapman & Hall, 1931).

Confessions of a Scoundrel [autobiography of a jewel thief, forger, burglar]. GEOFFREY SPENCER. (Werner Laurie, 1933).

Limey Breaks In [criminal career in England]. JAMES SPENSER. (Longmans, 1934).

Road Pirate: the Confessions of a Motor Bandit. EDDIE BROWNE. (John Long, 1934).

The Man who fooled a Continent. The Story of an amazing imposture. F. W. HARLAND-EDGCUMBE. (John Long, 1935).

B III—STUDIES IN SPECIFIC TYPES OF CRIME

B III 1 — MURDER [*See also* B I 2].

History of the Mysterious Murder [by WILLIAM CORDER] *of Maria Marten . . . in the Red Barn.* J. CURTIS. (London, Kelly, 1828). [Reprint in F II 2].

Infanticide: its law, prevalence, prevention and history. W. B. RYAN. (London, 1862).

Studies in Assassination. W. SIKES. (London, 1881).

Murder in all ages: being a history of homicide from the earliest times. MATTHEW W. PINKERTON. (Chicago, Pinkerton, 1898).

Noted Murder Mysteries. [Marie Lafarge and eight others]. PHILIP CURTIN [pseud., *i.e.*, MRS. BELLOC LOWNDES]. (Simpkin, Marshall, 1914, 1916).

The Criminal Imbecile: an Analysis of Three Remarkable Murder Cases. HENRY H. GODDARD. (New York, 1915).

Unsolved Murder Mysteries [under heads of gain, revenge, elimination, jealousy, love of killing, conviction]. CHARLES E. PEARCE. (Stanley Paul, 1924).

Murder and its motives [William Palmer, Constance Kent, de Querengals, Mrs. Pearcey, Neill Cream, Orsini]. F. TENNYSON JESSE [MRS. H. M. HARWOOD]. (Heinemann, 1924).

Studies in Murder. EDMUND LESTER PEARSON. (Macmillan, 1924).

Murder in Fact and Fiction. CANON J. A. R. BROOKES. (Hurst & Blackett, 1925).

Murder for Profit. W. BOLITHO. (Jonathan Cape, 1926).

Murder at Smutty Nose: containing the complete historical account of fourteen most amazing murders. [American; Louise Wagner, Prof. Webster, etc.]. EDMUND PEARSON. (Heinemann, 1927).

Riddles of Crime [14 unsolved murder mysteries]. ELIZABETH VILLIERS. (Werner Laurie, 1928).

Mass Murder. L. C. DOUTHWAITE. (John Long, 1928).

Masters of Crime: Studies of Multiple Murders. GUY B. H. LOGAN. (Stanley Paul, 1928).

Murder Most Foul: A Gallery of famous criminals. GEO. A. BIRMINGHAM [pseud., *i.e.*, JAMES OWEN HANNAY]. (Chatto & Windus, 1929).

Ten Real Murder Mysteries never solved. SIDNEY SUTHERLAND. (Putnam, 1929).

Rope, Knife and Chair [murder cases in Europe and America]. GUY B. H. LOGAN. (Stanley Paul, 1930; Rich & Cowan, 1933).

'*Thou shalt do no Murder.*' [Cases of Vaquier, True, Seddon, etc.]. ARTHUR LAMBTON. (Hurst & Blackett, 1930).

Black Cap; or Murder will out. W. and L. TOWNSEND. (Marrot, 1930).

Instigation of the Devil. [Twenty-five studies, mostly of murder, of celebrated crimes in England, France and United States]. EDMUND PEARSON. (Scribners, 1930).

Seven Murderers [includes Browne and Kennedy case]. CHRISTMAS HUMPHREYS. (Heinemann, 1931).

Great Murder Mysteries [15 cases]. GUY B. H. LOGAN. (Stanley Paul, 1931).

Murder by Persons Unknown [25 cases, including Dora Grey case of Yarmouth]. H. L. ADAM. (Collins, 1931).

Murders and Mysteries: A Canadian Series. W. S. WALLACE. (Toronto, Macmillan, 1931).

Homicide in the United States. H. C. BREARLEY. (Univ. of North Carolina Press; Oxford Univ. Press, 1932).

Murders and Murder Trials, 1812–1912. H. M. WALBROOK. (Constable, 1932, 1933).

Murder most Mysterious. [Benjamin Knowles, Ashanti, 1928; Louisa Maud Steele, Blackheath, 1929; Marjory Wren, 1930; Agnes Kesson, 1930; Evelyn Foster, 1931]. H. L. ADAM. (Sampson Low, 1932).

Enter Murderers: eight studies of Murder. EDWARD H. BIERSTADT. (Garden City, New York, U.S.A., Doubleday, Doran, 1934).

Up for Murder [19 South African Cases]. BENJAMIN BENNETT, with F. P. ROUSSEAU. (Hutchinson, 1934).

The Murder of the Romanovs. CAPTAIN PAUL BULYGIN. Foreword by ALEXANDER KERENSKY. (Hutchinson, 1935).

B III 2 — POISONING [*See also* E II 7].

Reports of Trials for Murder by Poisoning [Tawell, Palmer, etc.]. G. LATHOM BROWNE and C. G. STEWART. (Stevens, 1883).

The Poisoner of the Seventeenth Century, Marchioness de Brinvilliers. ALBERT SMITH. (London, 1886).

Princes and Poisoners [Court of Louis XIV.]. FRANTZ FUNCK-BRENTANO. Tr. by George Maidment. (Duckworth, 1901).

Poison Romance and Poison Mysteries. C. J. S. THOMPSON. (Scientific Press, 1902).

Mysteries of Police and Crime. Pt. VIII. on *Poisoners.* MAJOR A. GRIFFITHS. (Cassell, special edn., 3 vols., 1920).

Famous Poison Trials. H. EATON. (Collins, 1923, 1924).

Famous American Poison Mysteries. EDWARD H. SMITH. (Hurst & Blackett, 1927).

Poisons and Poisoners. C. J. S. THOMPSON, Curator, Hist. Section, Royal College of Surgeons. (Shaylor, 1931).

B III 3 — FRAUD.

Revelations of Facts, Failures and Frauds [banking and railway frauds]. D. MORIER EVANS. (London, Groombridge, 1861).

History of Monetary Crimes. A. DEL MAR. (New Jersey, Hackensack, 1901).

Insurance and Crimes. A. C. CAMPBELL. (Putnam, 1902).

The Literature of Roguery. F. W. CHANDLER. 2 vols. (Constable, 1907).

Famous Impostors [pretenders, practitioners of magic, witchcraft, hoaxes, etc.]. BRAM STOKER. (Sidgwick & Jackson, 1910).

The Romance of Fraud. TIGHE HOPKINS. (Chapman & Hall, 1914).

Everyday Swindles and how to avoid them. JOHN LAURENCE. (Pearson, 1921).

Liars and Fakers. PHILIP W. SERGEANT. (Hutchinson, 1925).

Library of Impostors : Narrative of the Life and Astonishing Adventures of John Daniel. Ed. M. M. Penzer. (Robert Holden, 1926).

Blackmailers and Co. J. C. ELLIS. (Selwyn & Blount, 1929).

Confidence Crooks and Blackmailers. BASIL TOZER. (Werner Laurie, 1929).

Princes of False Finance [bank frauds and forgery]. CHARLES CAREW. (Long, 1931).

Stacked Cards [on cardsharpers and confidence tricksters]. DAVE PHILLIPS. (Falcon Books, John Lane, 1934).

The Fire Raisers. [The Harris gang]. HAROLD DEARDEN. (Heinemann, 1934).

B III 4 — FORGERY [*See also* E II 3].

The Great Forgeries of William Roupell, 1862. (London, Vickers, 1862).

Forgery as a Profession. R. A. PINKERTON. (New York, 1894).

Trial of Henry Fauntleroy and some other famous Trials for Forgery. H. BLEACKLEY. (Hodge, 1924).

Crime in Ink. CLAIRE CARVALHO and BOYDEN SPARKES. (Scribners, 1929).

The Bank of England Forgery [1873 : George Bidwell, Austin Bidwell, G. Macdonnell, E. Noyes]. G. DILNOT. (The Famous Trials Series, G. Bles, 1929).

The Craft of Forgery. HENRY T. F. RHODES. (Murray, 1934).

B III 5 — HIGHWAY ROBBERY.

Lives and Exploits of English Highwaymen, Pirates and Robbers, drawn from the earliest and most authentic sources. C. WHITEHEAD. (Ball & Charton, 1846).

Half Hours with the Highwaymen : Picturesque Biographies and Traditions of 'Knights of the Road.' CHARLES G. HARPER. (Chapman & Hall, 1908).

Highwaymen. C. J. FINGER. (Harrap, 1925).

A Complete History of the Lives and Robberies of the Most Notorious Highwaymen. CAPT. ALEXANDER SMITH. (Reprint ; Routledge, 1926).

Brigands and Bandits. G. ROCCAPINO. (Drane, 1928).

Stand and Deliver [highwaymen]. ELIZABETH VILLIERS. (Stanley Paul, 1929).

The Highwaymen in Irish History. TERENCE O'HANLON. (Dublin, M. H. Gill, 1932).

Bandits Corses [Corsican]. MAURICE PRIVAT. (Paris, 1932).

B III 6 — PIRACY.

Buccaneers and Pirates of our Coasts. FRANK STOCKTON. (New York, 1898).

Buccaneers in West Indies in the 17th Century. C. H. HARING. (Methuen, 1910).

Buccaneers of the Spanish Main. A. M. HYAMSON. (Routledge, 1912).

A General History of the Pirates. CAPT. CHARLES JOHNSON. Ed. P. Gosse. 2 vols. (Cayme Press, 1925, 1926).

Corsairs: Sea Wolves of the Mediterranean. S. HAMILTON CURREY. (Nautilus Library, P. Allan, 1928).

Buccaneers of the Pacific. GEO. WYCHERLEY. (J. Long, 1929).

The Scourge of the Indies: Buccaneers, Corsairs and Filibusters. MAURICE BESSON. Tr. by E. Thornton. (Routledge, 1929).

The History of Piracy. PHILIP GOSSE. (Longmans, 1932).

Vampires of the China Coast. 'BOK.' (H. Jenkins, 1932).

B III 7 — ILLICIT TRAFFIC IN DRUGS.

The Black Candle [drug traffic and drug addiction]. MRS. EMILY F. MURPHY. (Toronto, Thomas Allen, 1922; London, Hurst & Blackett, 1926).

The Drug Traffic in the Punjab. F. L. NEWMAN. (*Police Journal*, Vol. III., p. 189, Jan. 1930).

Dangerous Drugs; the world fight against Illicit trade in narcotics. ARTHUR WOODS. (Yale Univ. Press; Oxford Univ. Press, 1931).

Reports of the Central Narcotics Intelligence Bureau, Egyptian Government, Cairo. (Cairo Govt. Press; annual).

Reports of the Narcotic Division, Dept. of Pensions and National Health, Dominion of Canada. (Ottawa; annual).

Inside Dope: An Exposure of the Drug Traffic. FERDINAND TUOHY. (Hamish Hamilton, 1934).

International Narcotic Control. L. E. S. EISENLEHR. (Allen & Unwin, 1935).

B IV—REGIONAL LITERATURE

B IV 1 — BRITISH EMPIRE [*See also* E III 2].

AFRICA, SOUTH.

Up for Murder. [Crime Stories for 1926-1932 in South Africa]. BENJAMIN BENNETT. (Hutchinson, 1934).

AUSTRALIA [*See also* TASMANIA].

Crime in New South Wales. H. H. HAYTER. (Melbourne, 1884).

Tales of Crime and Criminals in Australia. [Thirty years in the Penal Dept. of Victoria]. H. A. WHITE, formerly Governor of Ballarat Gaol. (Ward & Downey, 1894).

The Last of the Bushrangers: an account of the Capture of the Kelly Gang. F. A. HOARE, late Supt., Victorian Police. (Hurst & Blackett, 1894).

Story of the Australian Bushrangers. G. E. BOXALL. (Sonnenschein, 1899).

History of Australian Bushranging. C. WHITE. (Sydney, 1900).

Bushrangers. C. J. FINGER. (Harrap, 1925).

CANADA

Prevalence of Forgery in Canada. A. G. TAFT. (Canadian Banking Association, Vol. XX., p. 177, 1912).

A double murder in the Arctic Regions. INSPECTOR C. D. LA NAUZE, R.C.M.P. (*Police Journal*, Vol. II., p. 266, April, 1929).

Murder at Belly Butte and other Mysteries, from the records of the Mounted Police. T. MORRIS LONGSTRETH and HENRY VERNON. (Appleton, 1931).

INDIA: GENERAL

Murder made Moral: an account of the Thugs and other secret murderers of India. F. HOLLOCK. (Manchester, 1860).

Poisoners and their Craft. A. H. GILES. (*Calcutta Review*, Vol. lxxi., 1885).

Crime et folie chez les Hindous et les Birmans. E. LAURENT. (Paris, 1905).

Oriental Crime. H. L. ADAM. (Werner Laurie, 1908).

The Indian Criminal. H. L. ADAM. (J. Milne, 1909).

Cameos of Indian Crime: Studies of Native Criminality in India. H. J. A. HERVEY. (Stanley Paul, 1912).

Crime in India: A brief review of the more important offences included in the criminal returns. S. M. EDWARDES. (Oxford Univ. Press, 1925).

The Company of Cain. AL. CARTHILL [pseud., *i.e.*, B. C. H. CALCRAFT-KENNEDY]. (Blackwood, 1929).

Crime and Religious Belief in India. A. SOMERVILLE. 2 vols. (Calcutta, 1931).

Thug: a million murders [description of the suppression of thuggee by Sir W. H. Sleeman]. JAMES L. SLEEMAN. (Sampson Low, 1933).

Economic and Social Aspects of Crime in India. BIJOY SHANKER HAIKERWAL, Supt., Chunar Reformatory. (Allen & Unwin, 1934).

INDIA: BENGAL PRESIDENCY

Thieves and Swindlers. S. N. BANERJEA. (Calcutta, Indian Publishing Press, 1909).

Common Swindlers and Thieves' Tricks. Note of Warning to the Public. F. C. DALY. (Calcutta, 1915).

Manual of Criminal Classes operating in Bengal. F. C. DALY, Deputy Insp.-Gen. of Police. (Calcutta, Bengal Secretariat Press, 1916).

INDIA: BOMBAY PRESIDENCY

Notes of Criminal Classes in the Bombay Presidency. M. KENNEDY. (Bombay, Govt. Central Press, 1908).

Police and Crime in India. SIR E. G. COX. (Stanley Paul, 1911).

INDIA: MADRAS PRESIDENCY

Notes on Criminal Classes of the Madras Presidency. F. S. MULLALY. (Madras Govt. Press, 1892).

The History of Railway Thieves with hints on detection. M. PAUPA-RAO NAIDU. (Madras, Higginbotham, 1904, 1915).

The History of Professional Poisoners and Coiners of India. M. PAUPA RAO NAIDU. (Madras, 1904).

INDIA : UNITED PROVINCES

Serious Crime in an Indian Province ; being a record of the graver crime committed in the North West Provinces and Oudh [later United Provinces] *during eleven years, 1876–1886.* E. J. KITTS. (Bombay, Education Society's Press, 1889).

Report of Inter-provincial Crime, United Provinces, Bengal and Assam. P. B. BRAMLEY. (Allahabad, Govt. Press; 1904).

Indian Village Crimes [United Provinces], *with an Introduction on Police Investigation and confessions.* SIR CECIL WALSH. (Benn, 1929).

The Agra Double Murder. SIR CECIL WALSH. (Benn, 1929).

Crime in India [United Provinces], *with an Introduction on Forensic Difficulties.* SIR CECIL WALSH. (Benn, 1930).

Outlaws I have known, and other reminiscences of an Indian Judge [United Provinces]. SIR THEODORE PIGGOTT. (Blackwood, 1930).

INDIA : HEREDITARY CRIMINAL TRIBES

Illustrations of the History and Practices of the Thugs, and notices of some of the proceedings of the Govt. of India for the suppression of the crime of Thuggee. (London, W. H. Allen, 1837).

Report of Badhuk, alias Bagree, Dacoits and other Gang-robbers by Hereditary Profession. LT.-COL. W. H. SLEEMAN. (Calcutta, Bengal Military Orphan Press, 1843).

A Popular Account of the Thugs and Dacoits, the Hereditary Garotters and Gang-robbers of India. JAMES HUTTON. (London, Allen, 1857).

Notes on Criminal Tribes residing in or frequenting the Bombay Presidence, Berar and the Central Provinces. MAJOR E. J. GUNTHORPE. (Bombay, *Times of India* Press, 1882).

The Criminal Tribes of India [Madras]. M. PAUPA RAO NAIDU. (Madras, 1904).

The Criminal Tribes of the United Provinces. S. T. HOLLINS, Dt. Supt. of Police. (Allahabad, Govt. Press).

Modern Ishmaelites, or Sketches of the Wandering Tribes of the United Provinces. ARTHUR N. GORDON, Dt. Supt. of Police. (Allahabad ; *Pioneer* Press, 1905).

The Outlaws of Kathiawar and other Studies. C. A. KINCAID. (Bombay ; *Times of India* Press, 1905).

Some Criminal Tribes in India. G. W. GAYER. (Nagpur, Central Provinces Govt. Press, 1910).

The Outcasts [account of the Maghaya Domes]. G. [later SIR GEOFFREY] CLARKE. (Calcutta ; Thacker, Spink, 1913).

Crimincurology : being a review of the work of the Salvation Army among the Criminal Tribes of India, etc. F. BOOTH-TUCKER. (Simla, 1913, 1916).

Report on Questions relating to the Administration of Criminal and Wandering Tribes in the Punjab. HARI KISHUN KAUL and L. L. TOMKINS, Indian Police. (Lahore, Supt. Govt. Printing, 1914).

A Note on the Administration of criminal tribes in the Punjab, 1917–1919. (Lahore, 1920).

The Land Pirates of South India [Madras Presidency]. *An account of the Kuravers, a remarkable tribe of hereditary criminals.* W. J. HATCH. (Seeley, Service, 1928). [More properly, Kuravans].

History of the Criminal Tribes in the Madras Presidency. E. RAMACHANDRA SASTRI. (Madras, Sri Rama Press, 1930).

TASMANIA

Adventures of Martin Cash, comprising a faithful account of his exploits, while a bushranger under arms in Tasmania, in company with Kavanagh and Jones in the year 1843. Ed. J. L. Burke. (Hobart, 1870).

B IV 2 — EUROPE. [*See also* E III 3].

BELGIUM

La belgique criminelle. H. JOLY. (Paris, 1907).

La criminalité belge, 1868–1909. C. JACQUART. (Louvain, 1912).

FRANCE

Judicial Dramas, or the Romance of the French Criminal Law. HENRY SPICER. (Tinsley, 1872).

Des Homicides commis par les alienés. E. BLANCHE. (Paris, 1878).

L'Affaire Gouffé. DR. LACASSAGNE. (Lyon, 1891).

Studies of the French Criminals of the 19th Century [Lacenaive, Troppmann, and others]. H. B. IRVING. (Heinemann, 1901).

The Lyons Mail. A. EXOFFON. Tr. by R. G. Sherard. (Greening, 1903).
See also, L'Affaire du Courrier de Lyon [1793]. GASTON DELAYEN. (Paris, Education Nationale, 1905).

Dernes l'empoissoneur : une cause celèbre au xviiie siècle. G. CLARETIE. (Paris, 1906).

Celebrated Crimes. A. DUMAS. Ed. R. S. Gamell. 4 vols. [Vol. I., Borgias, etc. Vol. II., Urbain Grandier, etc. Vol. III., Marquise Brinvilliers, etc. Vol. IV., Ali Pacha, etc.]. (Methuen, 1907).

Four French Adventurers. STODDARD DEWEY. (Nelson, 1914).

Enigmes et Drames Judiciaires. G. A. PROVIEL. Tr. by D. Ashley. (Paris, Perrin, 1923).

Drames Judiciares d'autrefois. PIERRE BOUCHARDON. 4 vols. (Paris, Perrin, 1924–1928).

Criminal Paris. NETLEY LUCAS. Foreword by E. LOCARD. (Hurst & Blackett, 1926).

Passion, Murder and Mystery [annals of French crimes]. BRUCE GRAEME [pseud., *i.e.*, GRAHAM MONTAGUE JEFFRIES]. (Hutchinson, 1927).

Crime on the Continent [Marie Lafarge, Duke de Praslin ; also cases in Austria, Belgium, Germany, Italy, Russia and Switzerland]. HORACE WYNDHAM. (T. Butterworth, 1928).

Treasure and Tragedy [French crime]. GEORGE ADAM. (Cape, 1929).

Dramas of French Crime. RÉNÉ CASSELARI. (Hutchinson, 1930).

The Underworld of Paris. ALFRED MORAIN. (Jarrolds, 1930).

Secrets of the French Police. GEORGE DU PARCQ. (Jarrolds, 1934).

The Compleat Crook in France. FRANCIS D. GRIERSON. (T. Butterworth, 1934).

The Fateful Diamonds. [Period of Marie Antoinette]. JOCELYN RHYS. (Watts, 1934).

GERMANY

Continental Crimes [German and Austrian: cases of Col. Redl, Karl Hau, etc.]. E. L. VON SONNENBERG and O. TRETTIN, Berlin C.I.D. (Bles, 1935).

ITALY

La Camorra. G. ALONGI. (Turin, Bocca, 1890).

Il Romanzo di un Delinquente nato. N. ANTONIO. Ed. by A. G. Bianchi. (Milan, 1893).

Le Mafia e i Mafiosi. A. CUTRERA. (Palermo, 1900).

La Mafia; notas sobre la Criminalidad en Sicilia. EUGENE C. CALON. (Madrid, 1905).

Il Briganti celebre italiani. E. RONTINI. (Florence, 1911).

Mafia. S. MORASCA. (Rome, 1911).

The Camorra. TIBERINUS [pseud.]. (*Police Journal*, Vol. I., p. 361; July, 1928).

The Mafia. TIBERINUS [pseud.]. (*Police Journal*, Vol. III., p. 50; Jany., 1930).

Banditi, briganti e brigantesse nell' ottocenti. JACOPO GELLI. (Florence, 1931).

B IV 3.—AMERICA: UNITED STATES [*See also* A III 3 and E III 4].

The New York Tombs; its secrets and mysteries; being a history of noted criminals, with narratives of their crimes. C. SUTTON. (New York, 1874).

Criminals of America: Tales of the Lives of Thieves. P. FARLEY. (New York, 1876).

The Molly Maguires: the origin, growth and character of the organization. F. P. DEWEES. (Philadelphia, 1877).

The Jukes: A Study in Crime, Pauperism, Disease and Heredity. R. L. DUGDALE. (Putnam, 1877, 1884, 1886, 1895, 1910).

Homicide, North and South . . . . in . . . the United States. (Philadelphia, Lippincott, 1880).

The Dangerous Classes of New York and twenty years' work among them. CHARLES L. BRACE. (New York, Wynkoop & Hallinbeck, 1880).

The Professional Criminals of America. THOS. BYRNES, Chief of Detectives, New York City. (New York, Dillingham, 1886, 1895).

His own story of his eventful Life [gambler, burglar, safe-blower, etc.]. LANGDON W. MOORE. (Boston, 1893).

From Wall Street to Newgate, via Primrose Way. AUSTIN BIDWELL. (Hartford, Connecticut, 1895).

Tracy, the Bandit. W. B. HENNESSY. (Chicago, 1902).

The Autobiography of a Thief. ED. Hutchins Hapgood. (New York, Fox Duffield, 1903; London, Putnam, 1904).

From Boniface to Bank Burglar. GEORGE M. WHITE. (Bellows Falls, Vermont, U.S.A., 1905).

The Story of the Outlaw; a study of the Western desperado. E. HOUGH. (New York, Outing Pub. Co., 1907).

True Stories of Crime from the District Attorney's Office. ARTHUR TRAIN. (New York, Scribner, 1908).

Celebrated Criminal Cases of America [period 1830–1890]. THOMAS S. DUKE, Captain of Police. (San Francisco, James H. Barry Co., 1910).

Nation-Famous New York Murders. A. H. LOWIS. (New York, Dillingham, 1914).

Memoirs of the notorious Stephen Burroughs of New Hampshire. ROBERT FROST. (New York, MacVeagh, 1924; Cape, 1924–5).

Studies in Murder [American]. E. L. PEARSON. (Macmillan, 1924).

Keys to Crookdom [analytical survey of crimes and criminals]. GEORGE C. HENDERSON. (New York, Appleton, 1924).

The Crime and Trial of Leopold and Loeb. M. MCKERNAN. (Allen & Unwin, 1925).

You can't Win: the life story of a thief [American criminal]. JACK BLACK. (Macmillan, 1926).

The Gang: a study of 1313 gangs in Chicago. (Chicago, Univ. of Chicago Press, 1927).

Trigger Fingers [studies of American gunmen criminals]. OWEN P. WHITE. (New York, Putnam, 1927)'

Lockstep and Corridor [autobiography of a criminal]. CHARLES L. CLARK. Ed. Earle E. Eubanks. (Cincinnati, Streit, 1927).

Famous American Poison Mysteries. EDWARD H. SMITH. (Hurst & Blackett, 1928).

The Gangs of New York: an informal history of the underworld. HERBERT ASBURY. (Knopf, 1928).

Man's Grim Justice [Jack Callahan]. (Long, 1929).

Ten real murder mysteries [American]. SIDNEY SUTHERLAND. (Putnam, 1929).

Chicago May: her story. M. C. SHARPE. (Sampson Low, 1929).

The Confessions of a Gunman [gangster life in America]. DANNY AHEARN. (Routledge, 1930).

500 Criminal Careers. S. S. GLUECK and E. T. GLUECK. (New York, Knopf, 1930).

Look at Chicago. EDWARD D. SULLIVAN. (G. Bles, 1930).

The Crooks of the Waldorf. HORACE SMITH. (John Long, 1930).

Al Capone: the Biography of a self-made man [really an account of the Chicago gang system]. FRED D. PASLEY. (Faber & Faber, 1931).

Dynamite [class violence and racketeering in America]. LOUIS ADAMIC. (Cape, 1931).

Chicago Surrenders. EDWARD D. SULLIVAN. (G. Bles, 1931).

A Century of Gunmen: A Study in Lawlessness. FREDERICK WATSON. (I. Nicholson & Watson, 1931).

King Crime: An English study of America's greatest problem. COLLINSON OWEN. (Benn, 1931).

From Cain to Capone. JOHN MCCONAGHY. (New York, Brentano's, 1931).

Crime and the Criminal Law in the United States. HARRY BEST. (Macmillan, 1931).

The Sacco-Vanzetti Case. OSMUND K. FRAENKEL. (Routledge, 1931). *See also, The Untried Case—Sacco and Vanzetti and the Morelli gang.* HERBERT B. EHRMANN, one of the defence Counsel. (Hopkinson, 1935).

The Autobiography of a Criminal [Henry Tufts, an American, died 1931]. Ed. Edmund Pearson. (Jarrolds, 1931).

The Golden Age of Crime [in U.S.A.]. ARTHUR B. REEVE. (New York, Mohawk Press, 1931).

Oriental Crime in California, 1900–1927. (Stanford Univ. Press; Oxford Univ. Press, 1932).

Criminals and Politicians. DENIS T. LYNCH. (New York, Macmillan, 1932).

Homicide in the United States. H. C. BREARLEY. (Oxford Univ. Press, 1932).

Carrying a Gun for Al Capone [experiences of a gangster in the bodyguard of Al Capone]. JACK BILBO. (Putnam, 1932).

This Kidnapping Business [in U.S.A.]. EDWARD B. SULLIVAN. (John Lane, 1932).

Limey; an Englishman joins the Gangs [autobiography of a gunman]. JAMES SPENSER. Introduction by H. KINSGLEY LONG. (Longmans, 1933). *See also* B II 2.

Rough Stuff: the Life Story of a Gangster [' Goat Laven ']. (Falcon Series, John Lane, 1933).

An Englishman among the Gangsters. L. W. HOLMES. (Herbert Jenkins, 1933).

The Tragedy of Lynching [Southern Commission on the study of lynching]. ARTHUR F. RAPER. (Chapel Hill, Univ. of North Carolina Press, 1933).

The New World of Crime [12 American cases]. C. E. BECHHOFER ROBERTS. (J. Cape, 1933).

They took me for a Ride. GORDON FELLOWES [Criminal investigator]. (Allen & Unwin, 1934).

Muscling In [American racketeering]. FRED D. PASLEY. (Faber, 1934).

The Lindbergh Crime. SIDNEY B. WHIPPLE [Press reporter]. (Methuen, 1935).

Booze-Runner [liquor smuggling by land from Canada]. ' DEAN FIRTH.' (Sidgwick & Jackson, 1935).

PHILIPPINES

Criminality in the Philippine Islands. I. VILLAMOR. (Manila, 1909).

C. HISTORY AND MEMOIRS OF POLICE FORCES [*See also* D. *passim*].

C I — GENERAL

Index to the Police Forces of the British Empire, the U.S. America, and Foreign Countries. F. J. KIRCHNER. (1884). Revised by A. H. J. Kirchner and A. J. Abrams. (*Police Review* Pub. Co., 1931).

A Handy Guide to the Police Forces At Home and Overseas, including the Railway and Dock Police, the Women Police, the Colonial Police, and the Prison Service. (*Police Review* Pub. Co., 17th edn., 1934).

C II — GREAT BRITAIN AND IRELAND

ENGLAND AND WALES.

A History of Police in England. CAPTAIN W. L. MELVILLE LEE. [Describes the principles underlying the evolution]. (Methuen, 1901, 1903, 1905).

Short History of the Essex Constabulary. B. TARRUM. (Chelmsford, 1911).

Tort, Crime and Police in Mediaeval Britain, a Review of some Early Law and Custom. J. W. JEUDWINE. (London, Williams & Norgate, 1917).

Mysteries of Police and Crime. Pt. III. on *Police, Past and Present.* MAJOR A. GRIFFITHS. (Cassell ; special edition, 3 vols., 1920).

Scotland Yard [includes the history of the development of police in England]. SIR JOHN F. MOYLAN, Receiver, Metropolitan Police. (Putnams, 1928 ; 2nd edn., 1934).

The English Police : its Origin and Development. A short History of the English Police from the earliest times to the present day. E. H. GLOVER. (*Police Chronicle* Office, 1934).

CITY OF LONDON.

Watches in London, in John Stow's 'Survey of London.' (1593 ; reprint in Everyman's Library, Dent, 1912).

The Police of the City of London. JOHN STARK. (*Police Journal,* Vol. IV., p. 5, Jany., 1931 ; Vol. IV., p. 197, April, 1931).

PORT OF LONDON.

The Port of London Authority Police. W. H. A. WEBSTER. (*Police Journal,* Vol. III., p. 244, April, 1930).

METROPOLITAN POLICE.

See for *History* and *Administration* under one head in D II 3.

SCOTLAND.

Sketch of the history of the High Constables of Edinburgh ; with notes on the early watching . . . . and other police arrangements of the City. J. D. MARWICK. (Edinburgh, 1865).

Scottish Police in Early Times. PROF. R. [later SIR ROBERT] S. RAIT. (*Police Journal,* Vol. III., p. 79 ; Jany., 1930).

The Edinburgh City Police. RODERICK ROSS. (*Police Journal,* Vol. III., p. 498 ; Oct., 1930).

IRELAND.

The History of the Royal Irish Constabulary. R. CURTIS, County Inspector. (London, Simkin & Co., 1871).

Tales of the Royal Irish Constabulary. M. BROPHY. (Dublin, 1896).

In the Royal Irish Constabulary. G. G. GREEN. (London, 1905).

Report of the Commissions of Enquiry on the Royal Irish Constabulary and the Dublin Metropolitan Police, 1914. (H.M.S.O., 1914).

Report of the Viceregal Commission on the Reorganization and Pay of the Irish Police Forces. (H.M.S.O., 1920).

Terms of Disbandment of the Royal Irish Constabulary, 1922. (H.M.S.O., 1922).

C III—BRITISH EMPIRE

GENERAL.

The Police Services of the Empire. SIR JOHN CUMMING. (*United Empire*, Vol. XXI., p. 538; Royal Empire Society, 1930).

AFRICA, SOUTH.

The Mounted Police of Natal. H. P. HOLT. (Murray, 1910).

The Fighting Police of South Africa. J. E. M. T. ATTWELL. (Maritzburg, 1926).

Report of Commission of Enquiry . . . . into the organization of the South African Police Force, established under Act 14 of 1912. (Cape Town, 1926).

Autobiography of a Border Policeman [Bechuanaland and Matabeleland]. LT.-COL. H. LYNN STEVENS. (London, Witherby, 1927).

The Police Force of South Africa. Sub-Inspector F. W. COOPER. (*Police Journal*, Vol. II., p. 247; April, 1929).

Natal Mounted Police. COL. W. T. CLARKE. (*Police Journal*, Vol. IV., p. 337; July, 1931).

Black Frontiers [pioneer adventures with Rhodes Mounted Police in South Africa]. SAM KEMP. (Harrap, 1932).

South African Constabulary. Chap. VIII. of *Lessons from the Varsity of Life.* LORD BADEN POWELL. (Pearson, 1933).

Khaki and Blue. LT.-COL. R. S. GODLEY, late Deputy Commissioner, South African Police. (Lovat Dickson, 1935).

AUSTRALIA.

Black Police of Queensland: reminiscences of official work and personal adventures in the early days of the Colony. E. B. KENNEDY. (Murray, 1902).

The Trooper Police of Australia: A Record of Mounted Police Work in the Commonwealth from the earliest times of settlement to the present time. A. L. HAYDON. (A. Melrose, 1911).

Recollections of a Victorian Police Officer. J. SADLEIR. (Melbourne, 1913).

The New South Wales Police: a retrospect. JAMES MITCHELL. (*Police Journal*, Vol. II., p. 477; July, 1929).

The Birth and Early History of the New South Wales Police Force. HENRY BATESON. (*Police Journal*, Vol. VII., p. 112; Jany., 1934).

BORNEO, BRITISH NORTH.

The Constabulary of North Borneo. CAPT. W. C. ADAMS. (*Police Journal*, Vol. I., p. 310; April, 1929).

BURMA.

The Burma Military Police. CAPT. J. W. YOUNG. (*Police Journal*, Vol. I., p. 374; July, 1928).

CANADA.

Royal North-West Mounted Police: a corps history. E. J. CHAMBERS. (Montreal, Mortimer Press, 1906).

The Riders of the Plains. [A Record of the Royal North-West Mounted Police, 1873–1910]. A. L. HAYDON. (A. Melrose, 1910).

Mounted Police Life in Canada: a Record of Thirty-one Years' Service. CAPT. R. BURTON-DEANE. (Cassell, 1916).

Policing the Plains, being the Real-Life Record of the Famous Royal North-West Mounted Police. R. G. MACBETH. (Hodder & Stoughton, 1921).

A Policeman from Eton. CAPT. R. W. CAMPBELL. (Murray, 1923).

The Silent Force [R.C.M.P.]. T. MORRIS LONGSTRETH. (New York, Century Co., 1927; London, P. Allan, 1928). [Contains bibliography].

The Royal Canadian Mounted Police. COL. C. F. HAMILTON, R.C.M.P., Ottawa. (*Police Journal*, Vol. I., p. 641; Oct., 1928).

Policing the Top of the World [Ellesmere Island]. HERBERT P. LEE. (John Lane, 1928).

Pioneers of Justice. The story of the Royal Canadian Mounted Police. W. W. LIGGETT. (New York 1930).

A Mounty's Wife, being the Life Story of one attached to the Force, but not of it. LUTA MUNDAY. (Sheldon Press, 1930).

In Scarlet and Plain Clothes: the History of the Mounted Police. T. MORRIS LONGSTRETH. (Toronto, Macmillan, 1933).

To the Arctic with the Mounties. DOUGLAS S. ROBERTSON. (Toronto, Macmillan, 1934).

Get Your Man. [Experiences with the Royal North-West Mounted Police, 1907–1914]. BOB DYKER. (Sampson Low, 1934).

Under the Surface of Crime. Behind the scenes with a Police Officer. JACK BROWN. (Garden City Press, Gardenvale, Quebec Province, Canada, 1934).

CEYLON.

The Ceylon Police and its Development. H. [later SIR HERBERT] L. DOWBIGGIN. (*Police Journal*, Vol. I., p. 203; April, 1928).

CYPRUS.

The Development of the Police in Cyprus. LT.-COL. A. E. GALLAGHER, Chief Commandant. (*Police Journal*, Vol. I., p. 470; July, 1928).

GOLD COAST.

The Gold Coast Police. 'QUATAMBA.' (*Police Journal*, Vol. V., p. 94; Jany., 1932).

INDIA.

Reminiscences of an Indian Police official. [Bombay]. T. C. ARTHUR [pseud., *i.e.*, ARTHUR TRAVERS CRAWFORD]. (Sampson Low, 1894; Roxburgh Press, 1898).

Report of the Indian Police Commission, 1902–03. (H.M.S.O., Cmd. 2478, 1905).

A contribution to the History of the Police in Bengal. W. R. GOURLAY. (Calcutta, Bengal Govt. Press, 1916).

Life in the Indian Police [Bengal]. C. E. GOULDSBURY. (Chapman & Hall, 1922).

The Bombay City Police : a Historical Sketch, 1672–1916. S. M. EDWARDES. (Oxford University Press, 1924).

A history of the development of the police in the Punjab, 1849–1905. BARKAT RAM KALIA. (Punjab Govt. Record Office, 1929).

Modern India : Chap. VII., 'Law and Order.' SIR JOHN CUMMING. (Oxford University Press, 1931).

The Indian Police. J. C. CURRY [Indian Police, Bombay]. (Faber & Faber, 1932).

JAMAICA.

Story of a West Indian Policeman ; or 47 years in the Jamaica Constabulary. H. T. THOMAS. (Kingston, 1927).

The Jamaica Constabulary. Inspector W. P. C. ADAM. (*Police Journal*, Vol. V., p. 257 ; April, 1932).

MAURITIUS.

The Mauritius Police Force. F. R. G. ROUNTREE. (*Police Journal*, Vol. III., p. 50 ; Jany., 1930).

NIGERIA.

Sword and Spear. CAPTAIN F. H. MELLOR [includes period as Asst. Comr. of Police, Northern Nigeria]. (Selwyn & Blount, 1934).

PAPUA.

Armed Constabulary of Papua and its possibilities. W. N. BEAVER. (*Empire Magazine*, Vol. VIII., No. 5, p. 7 ; 1913).

The Armed Constabulary of Papua [New Guinea]. I. H. P. MURRAY. (*Police Journal*, Vol. IV., p. 571 ; October, 1931).

RHODESIA, SOUTHERN.

The British South Africa Police in Southern Rhodesia : history, present organization and work. LIEUT. J. H. STANLEY ADAM. (*Police Journal*, Vol. I., p. 553 ; October, 1928).

The Police Forces of Southern Rhodesia. LT.-COL. H. MARSHALL HOLE. (*Police Journal*, Vol. III., p. 435 ; July, 1930).

TRINIDAD.

The Trinidad Constabulary. COLONEL A. S. MAVROGORDATO. (*Police Journal*, Vol. V., p. 407 ; July, 1932).

C IV — EUROPE [*See also* D IV 1.]

AUSTRIA.

The Austrian Police. HOFRET DR. OSCAR DRESSLER. (*Police Journal*, Vol. II., p. 437 ; July, 1929).

Sechzig Jahre Wiener Sicherheitswache. [The Diamond Jubilee of the Vienna Constabulary]. HERR SCHOBER. (Vienna, 1929).

BELGIUM.

La Police Scientifique. E. GODDEFROY. (Ostende, 1911).

The Belgian Police. A. KEFFER and F E. LOUWAGE. (*Police Journal*, Vol. I., p. 443 ; July, 1928).

Denmark.

The Danish Police Forces. V. H. Mensen. (*Police Journal*, Vol. I., p. 240 ; April, 1928).

France.

La Police. L. Guyot. (Paris, 1884).

Paris Police. Charles Virmaitre. (Paris, E. Dentu, 1886).

Histoire du Corps des gardiens de la paix. Alfred Ray and L. Feron. (Paris, 1896).

Historique de l'institution des Commissaires de Police : son origine . . . . leur prérogatives. F. Euvrard. (Montpellier, 1910).

L'organisation de la Police en France. Etienne Felix Guyon. (Paris, 1923).

Histoire de la gendarmerie depuis ses origines de la maréchaussée jusqu' à nos jours. Louis Larrieu. New edn. (Paris, 1927).

La police municipale et rurale et les gardes champêtres. Emile Arnaud. (Paris, 1928).

The French Police : its Evolution from its Source to the Present Day. Pierre Guitet-Vauquelin. (*Police Journal*, Vol. I., p. 605 ; October, 1928).

Germany.

La Police Secrète Prussienne. Victor Tissot. (Paris, E. Dentu, 1884).

Die Berliner Polizei. Assessor. (Berlin, 1907).

Die Polizei aller Länder in Wort und Bild. Major Paul Riege, of Prussian Police Institute. (Dresden, Metro-Verlag, 1928). [Contains references to 25 countries ; but specially informative about police forces in Germany].

The Prussian Police. Paul Riege. (*Police Journal*, Vol. II., p. 225 ; July, 1929).

Holland.

Geschiedenis en inrichting der politie in Nederland. J. W. Haarman. (Alphen, 1922).

Hungary.

The Hungarian State Police. Dr. H. Dornung. (*Police Journal*, Vol. II., p. 62 ; Jany., 1929).

Italy.

The Vigiles of Imperial Rome. P. K. B. Reynolds. (H. Milford, 1926).

The Royal Carabiniers of Italy. Tiberinus [pseud.]. (*Police Journal*, Vol. I., p. 48 ; Jany., 1928).

Latvia.

The Latvian Police : the youngest European Police Force. Latvian Legation. (*Police Journal*, Vol. IV., p. 232 ; April, 1931).

Norway.

Kristiania Politis Historie. P. Holmsen. (Kristiania *i.e.* Oslo, 1884).

RUSSIA. [*See also* D IV 1].

The Russian Secret Police. J.R. (*Police Journal*, Vol. II., p. 492 ; July, 1929).

The Russian Secret Police. H. T. VASSELYEV, the late Tzarist Chief of Police. (Harrap, 1930).

Ogpu : The Russian Secret Terror. GEORGY S. AGABEKOV. Tr. from French by Henry W. Bunn. (New York ; Brentano's, 1931).

In the toils of the O.G.P.U. KARL KINDERMANN. Tr. by G. Griffin. (Hurst & Blackett, 1933).

SPAIN.

Policia Rural en España. L. REDONET Y LOPEZ-DORIGA. (Madrid, 1916).

The Spanish Civil Guard. LT.-GEN. DON JOSE SANJURJO, MARQUIS DEL RIF. (*Police Journal*, Vol. IV., p. 368, July, 1931 ; Vol. IV., p. 531, Oct., 1931).

C V — AMERICA

NORTH AMERICA : UNITED STATES. [*See also* D IV 2].

The Philadelphia Police, Past and Present. H. O. SPROGLE. (Philadelphia, 1887).

The Police of the District of Columbia. R. SYLVESTER. (Washington, Gibson, 1894).

Guarding a Great City. [New York]. WILLIAM MCADOO. (New York, Harper, 1906). [Historical account of the police system].

Justice to all : the history of the Pennsylvania State Police. KATHERINE MAYO. (New York ; Houghton, Mifflin, 1920).

The State Police in the United States. A Bibliography. MARGARET M. CORCORAN. (*Journal of the American Institute of Criminal Law and Criminology*, Vol. XIV., p. 544 ; 1924).

The State Police, organization and administration. BRUCE SMITH. (New York, Macmillan, 1925). [Contains select bibliography].

SOUTH AMERICA : ARGENTINA.

Historia de la Policia. LUIS J. ALBERT. (Buenos Aires, 1913).

C VI — ASIA

IRAQ.

The Iraq Police : a notable example of British administrative adaptability. LT.-COL. SIR ARNOLD T. WILSON. (*Police Journal*, Vol. I., p. 31 ; Jany., 1928).

JAVA.

The Dutch East Indian Police. A. HOORWEG. (*Police Journal*, Vol. II., p. 379 ; Oct., 1929).

PALESTINE [British Mandated Territory].

The Palestine Police Force under the Mandate. A. J. KINGSLEY HEATH, Dept. of Police and Prisons. (*Police Journal*, Vol. I., p. 78 ; April, 1928).

Sword for Hire [describes life in the British gendarmerie in Palestine]. DOUGLAS V. DUFF. (Murray, 1934).

SHANGHAI.

Shanghai : the International Settlement and the Municipal Police Force. BRIG.-GEN. C. D. BRUCE. (*Police Journal*, Vol. I., p. 128 ; Jany., 1928).

The Shanghai Municipal Police : Chinese Uniform Branch. MAJOR K. M. BOURNE. (*Police Journal*, Vol. II., p. 26 ; Jany., 1929).

SIAM.

A Sketch of Siam's gendarmerie. LIEUT.-COL. C. H. FORTY. (*Police Journal*, Vol. IV., p. 425 ; July, 1931).

D. POLICE ADMINISTRATION.

[*See also* C]

D I — GENERAL

Justice and Police. F. W. MAITLAND. (Macmillan, 1885).

De Polite in Frankrijk, Duitshland, Engeland en Nederland. J. BOOL. (The Hague, 1887).

The Police Code and the General Manual of the Criminal Law of the British Empire. COL. [later SIR] HOWARD VINCENT. (Cassell, 1881 ; Simpkin, Marshall, 1893 ; Butterworth, 1924). *Vincent's Police Code.* (Butterworth, 17th Edn., 1931 ; Shaw, 1931).

Police and Prison Encyclopaedia. G. W. HALE. (Boston, Richardson, 1894 ; also Eyre & Spottiswoode).

Office of Constable. H. B. SIMPSON. (*English Historical Review*, October, 1895).

The Police Power : public policy and constitutional rights. ERNST FREUND. (Chicago, Callaghan, 1904).

Police Administration : a critical study of police organization in the United States and abroad. L. F. FULD. (New York, Putnam, 1909, 1910).

The Police Encyclopaedia. H. L. ADAM. 8 Vols. (Routledge, 1911 ; Blackfriars Publishing Co., 1918 ; Waverley Book Co., 1920, 1925).

Police Work from within, with some reflections on Women, the Law and Lawyers. H. L. ADAM. (Holden & Hardingham, 1913, 1914).

European Police Systems. RAYMOND B. FOSDICK. (New York, Century Co. ; Allen & Unwin, 1915).

Policeman and Public. [Lectures on the responsibility of citizenship]. LT.-COL. ARTHUR WOODS [Police Commr., New York]. (Oxford University Press, 1920 ; Newhaven, U.S.A., Yale University Press, 1919).

Scotland Yard. [Discusses police systems of London, Paris, Berlin and Vienna]. JOSEPH GOLLOMB. (Hutchinson, 1926).

The Police and the Crime Problem. [Collection of articles by American and European police authorities on police organisation, personnel and investigation]. Ed. Thorsten Sellin. (American Academy of Political and Social Science, Concord, New Hampshire, 1929).

Report of the Royal Commission on Police Powers and Procedure. (Vol. I., Report ; Vol. II., Evidence ; Vol. III., Appendices. Cmd. 3297 ; H.M.S.O., 1929).

Police. Art. in 'Encyclopaedia of the Social Sciences,' Vol. XII. BRUCE SMITH. (Macmillan, 1934). [Contains bibliography].

D II — GREAT BRITAIN AND IRELAND

D II 1 — ENGLAND AND WALES. [*See also* D I & F VI 1, exclusive of Metropolis, for which *see* D II 3].

The Duty and Office of High Constables of Hundreds, Petty Constables, Tythingmen, and such inferior Ministers of the Peace. W. LAMBARD [later W. BROWN]. (London, 1677).

Observations upon the Office of Constable. SAUNDERS WELCH. (London, 1754).

The Constable's Assistant: a compendium of the Powers and Duties of Constables and other Peace officers. (London, 1808).

First Report of the Commissioners appointed to enquire as to the best means of establishing an efficient Constabulary Force in the Counties of England and Wales. (London, 1839).

Report of the Committee on the expediency of establishing a more uniform system of Police in England, Wales and Scotland. (London, 1853).

Snowden's Magistrates' Assistant and Police Officers' and Constables' Guide. 3rd Edn. Ed. J. F. Archbold. (London, 1857). 11th Edn. Ed. T. O. H. Lees and J. Ridley Shield. (Butterworth, 1905).

The Constable's Digest. [A treatise on police duty]. R. M. PRESCOTT. (London, Hamilton, 1889).

Criminal Life: Reminiscences of forty-two years as a police officer. J. BENT. (Manchester; J. Heywood, 1891).

Executive Power in relation to Crime and Disorder or Powers of Police in England. THOS. W. HAYCROFT. (Butterworth, 1897).

Reminiscences of a Chief Constable. [At Stalybridge]. WILLIAM CHADWICK. (Manchester; J. Heywood, 1900).

[Philip B.] *Bicknell's Police Manual.* Revised by E. G. M. Carmichael. (London, Knight, 1905).

English Local Government. SIDNEY and BEATRICE WEBB. (Longmans, 1906, 1908).

Die Polizei in Stadt und Land in Gross-brittanien. C. BUDDING. (Berlin, 1908).

Die Polizei als Grundlage und Organ der strafrechtspflege in England, Schottland und Irland. DR. KARL WEIDLICH. (Berlin, 1908).

Instructions for Liverpool City Police. L. [later SIR LEONARD] DUNNING. (Chief Constable). (Liverpool, 1911).

A Police Constable's Guide to his Daily Work. B. M. GREGG and J. C. MCGRATH. (Effingham Wilson, 1st Edn., 1912; 2nd Edn., 1915; 3rd Edn., 1919; 4th Edn., 1924). B. M. GREGG and J. E. LIGHTBURN (5th Edn., 1929). B. M. GREGG and C. P. BRUTTON. (6th Edn., 1931; Pitman, 7th Edn., 1934).

Handy Notes for Constables. J. T. GALLIMORE and J. STOTT. (Rotherham, 1914).

Police Systems in Urban Districts. A. LAW, Chief Constable, Hertfordshire. (King, 1919).

The Police Officer's A.B.C. LT.-COL. J. HALL-DALWOOD and F. J. O. CODDINGTON. (*Police Review* Pub. Co., 1920, 1924, 1927).

The Police Service of England and Wales. STANLEY SAVILL. (*Police Review* Pub. Co., 1923).

The Police Officer's Assistant. FRANK BUNN [Chief Constable]. (*Police Chronicle*, 1927; 4th Edn., 1934).

The Constable's Pocket Guide to Police Duty and Criminal Law. T. O. H. LEES. (Shaw, 1891. 17th Edn.; Ed. P. J. Sillitoe; Shaw, 1928).

Justice and Police in England. ALBERT LIECK, Chief Clerk, Bow Street Police Court. (Butterworth, 1929).

How to join the Police Force. (*Police Chronicle*, 1929).

Report of the Royal Commission on Police Powers and Procedure. (H.M.S.O., 1929).

Helpful Talks for young Police Officers. JOHN WILLIAMSON, Chief Constable, Northampton. (*Police Chronicle*, 1930).

A Manual of Criminal Law and Criminal Procedure for Police. E. W. PUTTKAMMER. (Cambridge Univ. Press, 1931).

Lincolnshire Constabulary Instruction Book. Compiled by W. TRIGG. (Lincoln, 1931).

Police Procedure and Administration. C. C. H. MORIARTY, Asst. Chief Constable, Birmingham. (Butterworth, 1931 ; 2nd Edn., 1933).

The Internal Police Administration of England. HAROLD BENJAMIN. (*Police Journal*, Vol. IV., p. 438 and p. 598 ; July and Oct., 1931).

The Coroner's Officer's Guide. A complete handbook for police officers preparing for and attending coroners' inquests. ARTHUR H. NEVE, Coroner for Kent. (Tonbridge, Free Press, 1935).

D II 2 — CITY OF LONDON.

From Constable to Commissioner. LT.-COL. SIR HARRY SMITH, at one time Commissioner, City Police. (Chatto & Windus, 1910).

Fifty-Two years a Policeman. SIR WILLIAM NOTT-BOWER, Commissioner, City Police. (Arnold, 1923).

The Police of the City of London. JOHN STARK. (*Police Journal*, Vol. IV., p. 5, Jany., 1931 ; Vol. IV., p. 197, April, 1931).

D II 3 — METROPOLITAN AREA [includes SCOTLAND YARD].

Watch in London in John Stow's 'Survey of London.' (London, 1598 ; reprint in Everyman's Library, Dent, 1912).

Observations on the practice of a Justice of the Peace intended for such gentlemen as intend to act for Middlesex and Westminster. SIR THOMAS DE VEIL. (London, 1748).

Enquiry into the Causes of the Late Increase of Robbers, with some proposals for remedying this growing evil. HENRY FIELDING. (London, 1751).

Plan for preventing robberies within twenty miles of London. SIR JOHN FIELDING. (London, 1753).

Account of the origin and effects of a Police set on foot by His Grace the Duke of Newcastle in 1753 upon a plan presented to His Grace by the late Henry Fielding. SIR JOHN FIELDING. (London, 1755).

The London and Westminster Police Bill, of Sir Archibald Macdonald, Solicitor General. [Not passed into Law]. (London, 1785).

A Treatise on the Police of the Metropolis. DR. P. COLQUHOUN. (Fry, London, 1796, 1797, 1800). [Led to founding of the "Marine Police" in 1798].

The Commerce and Police of the River Thames. DR. P. COLQUHOUN. (London, 1798. 1800).

Report of the Select Committee of the House of Commons for the establishment of a New Police of the Metropolis. (London, 1799).

Report of the Committee of 1812. (London, 1812).

Reports of the Committee of 1816-18. (London, 1817 and 1818).

Observations on the Present State of the Police of the Metropolis. GEO. B. MAINWARING. (London, 1821).

Brief Considerations on the Present State of the Police of the Metropolis : with a few suggestions towards its improvement. G. H. B. ALLEN. (London, 1821).

Report of the Committee appointed by Sir Robert Peel as Home Secretary. (London, 1828).

Metropolitan Police Improvement Act, of 19th June, 1829: 10 Geo. IV., c. 44. (London, 1829).

Metropolitan Police Act. [Absorbed the Thames River Police]. (London, 1839).

Metropolitan Police Manual. JOHN STONE. 2nd Edn. (Shaw & Sons, 1839).

The Police Force of the Metropolis in 1868. CUSTOS [pseud.]. (London, 1868).

Police. [Refers to Metropolitan Police]. C. T. CLARKSON and J. H. RICHARDSON. (Simpkin, Marshall, 1889). [Collaboration of police officer and journalist].

Scotland Yard, Past and Present. T. A. CAVANAGH. (London, 1893).

Instruction Book for the Government and Guidance of the Metropolitan Police Force. SIR EDWARD R. C. BRADFORD, Comr. of Police. (H.M.S.O., 1900).

The Metropolitan Police Guide: being a compendium of the law affecting the Metropolitan Police. W. F. A. ARCHIBALD, T. H. GREENHALGH and J. ROBERTS. (Eyre & Spottiswoode, 1906, 1922).

Report of the Royal Commission on the Metropolitan Police. (London, H.M.S.O., 1908).

The Metropolitan Police. J. P. BLAND. (*The Times* Office, 1909).

The London Police from a New York Point of View. WM. MCADOO, Police Comr. of New York. (*Century Magazine*, Sept., 1910).

Life of Sir Howard Vincent, Director, C.I.D. Metropolitan Police. S. H. JEYS and F. D. HOW. (G. Allen, 1912).

Scotland Yard: the methods and organisation of the Metropolitan Police. G. DILNOT. (London; Perceval, Marshall, 1915).

Annals of an Active Life. SIR NEVIL MACREADY, once Comr., Metropolitan Police. (Hutchinson, 1924).

The Story of Scotland Yard. [Growth; organisation]. G. DILNOT. (Geoffrey Bles, 1926, 1930).

Scotland Yard and the Metropolitan Police. J. [later SIR JOHN] F. MOYLAN, Receiver, Metropolitan Police. (Whitehall Series, Putnam, 1928; 2nd edn., 1934).

Police Reform before Peel. J. [later SIR JOHN] F. MOYLAN. (*Police Journal*, Vol. II., p. 150; Jany., 1929).

The Port of London Authority Police. W. H. A. WEBSTER. (*Police Journal*, Vol. III., p. 244; April, 1930).

C.I.D. or Behind the Scenes at Scotland Yard. [Lord Byng, finger prints, etc.]. H. L. ADAM. (Sampson Low, 1931).

The History of the Criminal Investigation Department at Scotland Yard. MARGARET PROTHERO. (Jenkins, 1931).

The History of the Bow Street Runners. [1729-1829]. GILBERT ARMITAGE. (Wishart, 1932).

Reports of the Commissioner of Police of the Metropolis for the years 1932 and 1933. [Lord Trenchard's Reports]. (H.M.S.O.; Cmd. 4294 and Cmd. 4562; 1933 and 1934).

Memorandum on the subject of certain changes in the Organisation and Administration of the Metropolitan Police. [Lord Trenchard's Reforms]. (H.M.S.O.; Cmd. 4320, 1933).

Metropolitan Police Act, 1933. (23 & 24 Geo. V. Ch. 33; H.M.S.O., 1933).

The Life and Work of Sir John Fielding. R. LESLIE-MITCHELL. (Lincoln Williams, 1934).

Secrets of Scotland Yard. [History of New Scotland Yard and the Police Force, with account of training and problems]. EDWIN T. WOODHALL. (John Lane, 1935).

D II 4 — SCOTLAND.

Police Manual, compiled by a Committee of Chief Constables in Scotland. (MacCorquodale, Glasgow, 1893).

A Treatise on the Powers and Duties of Police Constables in Scotland. J. W. ANGUS. (Edinburgh, 1922).

The Law and Practice relating to Municipal and Police Government in Burghs in Scotland. J. MUIRHEAD. 2 Vols. (Edinburgh, 1924).

What a Policeman should know. RODERICK ROSS, Chief Constable, Edinburgh. (*Police Chronicle* Publishing Dept., 1926).

Scottish Police Administration in Town and Country. DONALD A. ROSS. (*Police Journal*, Vol. III., p. 412 ; July, 1930).

D II 5 — NORTHERN IRELAND.

Royal Ulster Constabulary Constables' Guide. W. ATTERIDGE. (Dublin, Thom, 1934).

IRISH FREE STATE.

The Garda Siochana Guide. MICHAEL HORGAN AND PATRICK CARROLL. (Dublin, Thom, 1934).

D II 6 — SPECIAL CONSTABLES.

The Special Constable : his duties and privileges. (Pearson, 1914).

An elementary guide to the duties of a special constable. J. A. BATTLEY. (Harrogate, 1918).

Two years with the Specials. SUB-INSPECTOR. (Crowther & Goodwin, 1916).

All Clear. A brief account of the work of the London Special Constabulary, 1914-1919. (London, Everett, 1920).

The Specials ; how they served London : the story of the Metropolitan Special Constabulary. W. T. REAY. (Heinemann, 1920).

City of London Police Reserve—A record, 1914-1920. (London, 1921).

The Metropolitan Special Constabulary. COL. W. T. REAY. (*Police Journal*, Vol. I., p. 317 ; April, 1928).

The City of Edinburgh Special Constabulary. JAMES STEUART. (*Police Journal*, Vol. II., p. 485 ; July, 1929).

D II 7 — THE POLICE FEDERATION.

Police Act, 1919 : sec. 1 and Schedule Pt. I. (H.M.S.O., 1919).

The Genesis, Scope and Aims of the Police Federation System of England and Wales. J. M. BRANTHWAITE, Chairman of Joint Central Committee. (*Police Journal*, Vol. I., p. 19 ; Jany., 1928).

Metropolitan Police Act, 1933 ; sec. 3. (H.M.S.O., 1933).

Memorandum on Changes in the Organisation and Administration of the Metropolitan Police. Appendix IV. (Cmd. 4320 ; H.M.S.O., 1933).

D III — BRITISH EMPIRE

D III 1—GENERAL.

The Police Services of the Empire. Unity amid Diversity. SIR JOHN CUMMING. (*United Empire*, Journal of the Royal Empire Society ; Oct., 1930).

Imperial Policing. [Deals with the utilization of the Army in support of the regular Police Forces]. MAJOR-GENERAL SIR CHARLES W. GWYNN. (Macmillan, 1934)

A Handy Guide to the Police Forces At Home and Overseas. 17th Edn. (*Police Review* Pub. Co., 1934).

D III 2 — INDIA [*See also* C III].

Report of the Committee to draw up a plan for the more efficient organization of the Mofussil [*i.e.* provincial] *Police.* (Calcutta, 1837-38).

Selections from the Government Papers relating to the Reform of the Police of India. (Calcutta, 1861).

The Police Officer's Manual. KABAD RAM RAO. (Madras Govt. Press, 1869).

Questions and Answers on Police Duties. G. E. FRYER. (Rangoon, 1887).

Manual for the Instruction of Constables in their duties. W. SWAIN. (Bengal Govt. Press, Calcutta, 1903).

Report of the Indian Police Commission on ***1902-03.*** (H.M.S.O., 1905).

Police Training School Manual. W. A. KNYVETT. (Bengal Govt. Press, 1908).

Stepping Stones to Police Efficiency. W. A. GAYER. (Allahabad, Pioneer Press, 1909).

The Indian Policeman. ZAFAR OMAN, Deputy Supt. of Police, United Provinces. (Delhi, 1913).

Glimpses of Police Work in Tinnevelly [S. India]. D. J. WINIFRED. (Madras, 1914).

The Control of Professional Crime. G. P. WHALLEY. (Calcutta, Thacker, 1919).

Practical Methods of Police Work. H. R. WARNER AND MUNSHI SAFDAR HUSAIN. (Allahabad, 1020).

The Bombay City Police. S. M. EDWARDES. (Oxford Univ. Press, 1924).

The Indian Police. J. C. CURRY, Indian Police [Bombay]. (Faber & Faber, 1932).

JAMAICA.

The Sub-Officers' Guide. HARRY MACCREA. 5th Edn. ED. C. H. Yorke-Slader. (Kingston, Jamaica ; Gleaner Co., 1924).

SOUTH AFRICA.

Policeman's Manual and General Outline of Methods of Police Work. JAMES HOPE [Bechuanaland Protectorate Police]. (Cape Town ; Juta & Co., 1934).

D IV — REGIONAL LITERATURE

D IV 1 — EUROPE.

BELGIUM.

The Belgian Police. A. KEFFER and F. E. LOUWAGE. (*Police Journal,* Vol. I., p. 443 ; July, 1928).

FRANCE.

[*See also* C IV]

Historie de l'administration de la Police de Paris. M. FRÉGIER. (Paris, Guillaumin, 1850).

La Police. YVES GUYOT. (Paris, Charpentier, 1884).

Dictionnaire Général de police administrative et judiciaire. FELIX BRAYER. 4 Vols. (Paris, 1886-90, 1907).

Le Service de la Sûreté. Par son ancien Chef [GUSTAV MACÉ]. (Paris, Charpentier, 1887).

Notions générales de police, organisation de la police en France, police administrative, préfecture de police. Ed. Paul Dupont. (Paris, 1905).

Traité théorique et pratique de droit pénal français. PIERRE GARRAUD. (Paris, Larose et Tenin, 1913).

Contribution à l'organisation de la Police. R. A. REISS. (Paris, Payot, 1914).

La police, ce qu'elle est, ce qu'elle devant être. E. LOCARD. (Paris, Payot, 1919).

Les projets gouvermentaux de réorganisation de la Police. A. LASSERRE. (Rennes, Thèse, 1920).

Manuel élémentaire de police technique. E. GODDEFROY. (Paris, Godde, 1922).

L'organisation de la Police en France. ETIENNE FELIX GUYON. (Paris, 1923).

Traité de Police. GASTON AREXY. (Paris, Dalloz, 1925).

Actes du premier Congrès de police judiciaire. [Monaco, 1914]. Ed. M. ROUX. (Paris, Godde, 1926).

La police française ; organisation ; technique. (Paris, 1926).

Ce qu'il faut connaître de la Police et ses mystères. LEON AMELINE. (Paris, Boivin, 1926).

Mes Souvenirs. M. LEPINE, Préfet de Police, Paris. (Paris, Payot, 1929).

The French Police from Within. RENÉ FARALICQ [formerly Commissaire]. (Cassell, 1933).

Trente Ans dans les rues de Paris. GASTON FARALICQ. (Paris, Perrin, 1934).

GERMANY.

Unser Polizeiwesen. FRANZ LAUFER. (Stuttgart, 1906).

Gross-stadtpolizei : ein praktisches handbuch der deutschen Polizei. GUSTAV ROSCHER. (Hamburg, 1912).

The Prussian Police. POLICE MAJOR PAUL RIEGE. 3rd Edn. (Berlin, C. A. Weller, 1932).

ITALY.

Manual di Polizia Scientifica. G. ALONGI, Ispettore di Pubblica Sicurezza. (Societa Editrice Souzogno, Milan, 1898).

RUSSIA. (*See also* C IV)

The Tcheka : the Red Inquisition. GEORG POPOV. (A. M. Philpot, 1925).

In the Clutches of the Tcheka. BORIS CEDERHOLM. Tr. by F. H. Lyon. (Allen & Unwin, 1929).

The Methods of the Ogpu, the secret Police Organization of Soviet Russia. VLADIMIR BRUNOVSKY. (Harpers, 1931).

Soviet Administration of Criminal Law. J. ZELITCH. (Pennsylvania Univ. Press, 1931 ; Oxford Univ. Press, 1932).

The Ochrana, the Russian Secret Police. A. I. VASILEV. (Harrap, 1932).

D IV 2—AMERICA ; UNITED STATES.

Treatise on the limitations of Police Power in the United States. C. G. TIEDEMAN. (St. Louis, Thomas, 1887).

Police Administration : a critical study of police organizations in the United States and abroad. L. F. FULD. (New York, Putnam, 1909, 1910).

American Police Systems. RAYMOND B. FOSDICK. (New York, Publications of the Bureau of Social Hygiene ; Century Co., 1920).

American Police Administration: a Handbook on Police organization and Methods of Administration in American Cities. Elmer D. Graper. (New York, Macmillan, 1921).

The Policeman. Cornelius F. Cahalane. (New York, Dutton, 1923).

The State Police: Organization and Administration. [Contains bibliography]. Bruce Smith. (New York, Macmillan, 1925).

The Policeman's Manual: a standard guide to the latest methods and duties. G. F. Chandler. (New York, 1930).

Report on Lawlessness in Law Enforcement. (National—Wickersham—Commission on Law Observance and Enforcement, No. 11; Washington, U.S. Govt. Printing Office, 1931).

Our Lawless Police: a study of the unlawful enforcement of the law. Ernest Jerome Hopkins. (New York, Viking Press, 1931).

Report of the Wickersham Commission on the Police of the U.S. America. (National Commission on Law Observance and Enforcement, No. 14; Washington, U.S. Govt. Printing Office, 1931).

Chicago Police Problems. By the Citizens Police Committee. (Chicago Univ. Press; Cambridge Univ. Press, 1931).

Rural Crime Control. Bruce Smith. (National Institute of Public Administration; New York, Columbia University, 1933).

Private Police. [Examination of private police in railways and in industries in America]. Dr. J. P. Shalloo. (Philadelphia, American Academy of Political and Social Science, 1933).

Police. Art. in 'Encyclopaedia of the Social Sciences,' Vol. XII. Bruce Smith. (Macmillan, 1934).

Police Administration in Boston. Leonard V. Harrison. (Cambridge, Mass., Harvard Univ. Press, 1934; Oxford Univ. Press, 1935).

D V — TRAFFIC OFFENCES AND TRAFFIC CONTROL.

The Law of Collisions on Land. Judge R. O. Roberts and A. D. Gibb. (Sweet & Maxwell, 1925, 1929).

Fundamentals of Highway Traffic Regulation. W. P. Eno. (Washington, U.S.A.; Eno Foundation for Highway Traffic Regulation, 1926).

The Traffic Problem. F. J. Crawley, Chief Constable, Newcastle-upon-Tyne. (Newcastle Central Police Station Printing Press, 1930).

Road Traffic. W. T. Hutchison. (*Police Review* Pub. Co., 1930). [Supplements later].

Road Traffic Law. F. Llewellyn Jones. (Sweet & Maxwell, 1930).

Digest of the Law of the Regulation of Traffic. H. Pearson [Inspector]. (*Police Review* Pub. Co.).

Road Traffic Act, 1930. Ed. R. P. Mahaffy and G. Dodson. (Butterworth, 1930).

Traffic Officers' Training Manual. C. P. Taylor. (Chicago National Safety First Council, 1930).

Rules and Regulations under the Road Traffic Act, 1930. Ed. R. P. Mahaffy and G. Dodson. (Butterworth, *1931*).

The Law of Running Down Cases. E. Terrell. (Butterworth, 1931).

European Conference on Road Traffic, 1931. [Held at Geneva, 1931]. (Boston, World Peace Foundation, 1931).

Impressions of American Traffic Conditions. GILBERT CARMICHAEL. (*Police Journal*, Vol. VI., p. 322 ; July, 1933).

Street Traffic Flow. HENRY WATSON. (Chapman & Hall, 1933 ; 2nd Edn., 1935.) [Contains bibliography].

*A bibliography of street traffic control in American Cities, **1920-1933**.* ALBERT RUSSELL ERSKINE Bureau for Street Traffic Research, Harvard University. (Cambridge, U.S.A. ; Harvard University, 1934).

[E. Gilbert] *Woodward's Road Traffic Acts and Orders, **1930-1934**.* (Eyre & Spottiswoode, 1934).

Publications of the National Safety First Association. (London, 52, Grosvenor Gardens, S.W.1.).

The Police and Traffic Control, chap. XII. of 'Scotland Yard.' SIR JOHN MOYLAN. (2nd Edn. ; Putnam, 1934).

Automatic Street Traffic Signalling. H. H. HARRISON and T. R. PREIST. (Pitman, 1934).

*Road and Rail Traffic Law, **1934**.* R. P. MAHAFFY and JUDGE GERALD DODSON. (Butterworth, 1934).

Some Modern Traffic Problems. A. MATHESON, Ministry of Transport. (*Police Review,* July 12, 1935).

D VI — MOUNTED POLICE.

The Metropolitan Mounted Police. E. P. BURRELL BAGGALAY. (*Cavalry Journal,* Royal United Service Institution ; Jany. and April, 1929).

Mounted Police in India. C. R. PETERS. (*Police Journal,* Vol. IV., p. 100 ; Jany., 1931).

D VII — WOMEN POLICE.

Report of the Departmental Committee on the Employment of Police Women. (H.M.S.O., 1924).

The Policewoman, her service and ideals. MRS. MARY E. HAMILTON. (New York, Stokes, 1924).

The Pioneer Policewoman. MARY S. ALLEN. (Chatto & Windus, 1925).

Weibliche Polizei, ihr werden, ihre ziele und arbeitsformen. J. ERKENS. (Lübeck, 1925).

Women Police : a study of the development and status of the women police movement. CHLOE OWINGS. (New York, Hitchcock, 1925).

Women Police Abroad. EDITH TANCRED., (*Police Journal,* Vol. IV., p. 175 ; April, 1931).

The Policewoman's Handbook. ELEONORE L. HUTZEL [Deputy Comr., Detroit Police Dept.] and MADELEINE L. MACGREGOR. (New York, Columbia Univ. Press, 1931 ; London, Oxford Univ. Press, 1933).

D VIII — TRAINING OF OFFICERS AND MEN : SCHOOLS AND COLLEGES.

Police Training School Manual [in Bengal and Bihar Provinces, India]. W. A. KNYVETT. (Calcutta, Bengal Govt. Press, 1908).

The Bengal Police Training College Manual. (Calcutta ; Bengal Secretariat Book Depot, 1913).

The Police Training College Manual, Phillaur [Punjab]. (Lahore; Supt. Govt. Printing, Punjab, 1915).

The Policeman's Art as taught in the New York State School for Police. George F. Chandler. (New York, Funk, 1922).

The Police Training School Manual for Burma. (Rangoon; Supt. Govt. Printing, Burma, 1925).

The Training of an East African Policeman [Kenya Colony practice]. C. I. Sempill. (*Police Journal*, Vol. I., p. 669; Oct., 1928).

The Prussian Police [includes Police Schools and Police Institute]. Paul Riege, Police Institute. (*Police Journal*, Vol. II., p. 225; April, 1929).

Some Aspects of Training for Police Service [in New York State and New York City]. Arthur Woods. (*Police Journal*, Vol. II., p. 355; July, 1929).

The Police Recruit [practice at Birmingham, England]. C. C. H. Moriarty. (*Police Journal*, Vol. II., p. 453; July, 1929).

The Primary Course in the Education and Training of the Police Officer [in the State of Oregon, U.S.A.]. Capt. H. M. Niles, Supt. Police Dept. (*Police Journal*, Vol. II., p. 529; Oct., 1929).

The New York Police College. Grover A. Whalen, late Police Comr. (*Police Journal*, Vol. III., p. 342; July, 1930).

Glasgow Police Training School. J. Hunter. (*Police Journal*, Vol. IV.; July, 1931).

Bibliography on the Training of Police. D. Campbell. (Chicago, Journal of the American Institute of Criminal Law and Criminology, Vol. XXIV., p. 591).

The Palestine Police Constable's Manual. A. J. Kingsley Heath, O.C., Training School, Palestine Police. (Jerusalem, Goldberg's Press, 1931).

D IX — PERIODICALS DEALING WITH POLICE FORCES OR POLICE MATTERS [*See also* E II 8]

1.—England.

Justice of the Peace and Local Government Review. (7, Fetter Lane, E.C.4, London; weekly).

Nottingham City Police Magazine. (Nottingham).

On and Off Duty. Organ of the International Christian Police Association [founded by Miss Gurney in 1882]. (117, Victoria Street, S.W.1, London; monthly).

Police Chronicle and Constabulary World. (53 Fleet Street, E.C.4, London; weekly).

Police Journal. (London, Philip Allan; quarterly).

Police Review. (5, Red Lion Square, W.C.1, London; weekly).

Policewoman's Review. (68, Victoria Street, S.W.1, London; monthly).

The Truncheon. (Essex Constabulary, Chelmsford).

Scotland.

The Scottish Constable; a monthly magazine devoted to the interests of the Scottish Police. (Glasgow; from 1933).

Ireland.

Royal Ulster Constabulary Review. (Belfast).

See also under Irish Free State.

D IX 2 — BRITISH EMPIRE.

(a) Dominions.

Union of South Africa.

The Nongqai [*i.e.* armed watchman (Bantu)]. *The South African Forces Magazine.* (New Government Buildings, Pretoria, South Africa; monthly).

Commonwealth of Australia.

New South Wales Police News: the official organ of the New South Wales Police Association. (Tomalin & Wigmore, 1-3, Goulburn St., Sydney, New South Wales; monthly).

Police News and official organ of the W.A. Police Association. (H. C. Gardner, 32, Angove St., North Perth, West Australia).

Queensland Police Union Journal. (Moreton Printing Co., Ann St., Brisbane).

Dominion of Canada.

Canadian Police Bulletin: organ of the Chief Constables' Association of Canada. (385, Sackville St., Toronto, Canada; quarterly).

Canadian Police Gazette: a magazine devoted to the explanation of police activities in Canada. (P.O. Box 174, Vancouver, B.C., Canada; monthly).

The Police Patrol: official organ of the Toronto Police Association. (Toronto).

Irish Free State.

The Garda Review: the organ of the Garda Siochana [Civic Guard]. (Dublin; A. Thom & Co., 2, Crow St.; monthly).

(b) Colonies.

Ceylon.

Off Duty: a magazine for members of the Ceylon Police Force. (Colombo).

Malaya.

Malayan Police Magazine. (Kuala Lumpur, F.M. States; monthly).

D IX 3 — EUROPE.

Belgium.

Revue Belge de la police administrative et judiciare. (180, rue Americaine, Brussels; monthly).

Czechoslovakia.

Vestnik. (Prague).

France.

Revue de la Gendarmerie. (C. Lavauzelle et Cie, 124 boulevard Saint-Germain, Paris).

La Voix des Polices [organ of the Syndicat National of the Police of France and the Colonies]. (Paris; fortnightly).

Germany.

Der Born: Zeitschrift für die Ausbildung .... Polizeibeamten. (Dresden; Metro-Verlag; weekly).

Deutsche Polizei Archiv. (Deutschen Polizei Verlag; half monthly).

Die Polizei Praxis. Halbmonatsschrift der vereinigung für polizeiwissenschaftliche fortbildung. (Berlin; half-monthly).

Die Polizei; Zeitschrift für die gesamte Polizei-u-Kriminalwesen mit einshluss der Landjägerei. (Berlin; fortnightly).

Die Polizeifachkunde: Zeitschrift für die Ausbildung . . . Polizeibeamten. (Dresden; monthly).

Die Preussische Schutzpolizei; Zeitschrift des Verbandes der Schulzpolizeibeamten Preussens. (Berlin; fortnightly).

Polizei im Bild. (Dresden, Metro-Verlag; monthly).

HOLLAND.

Tijdschrift voor de Politie. (Amsterdam; quarterly).

HUNGARY.

Csendörsegi Lepok sycrkesztösége. (Budapest, Országhaz-utca 30).

ITALY.

Rivista di Polizia: Supplemento mensile al giornale 'La Tutela Pubblica'. (Rome, via Muzio Clementi, 45-47; monthly).

NORWAY.

Medlemsbad for Politiembedsmennenes Landsforening. (Oslo; bi-monthly).

D IX 4 — AMERICA: UNITED STATES.

The Police Journal [unofficial]. (Police Journal Publishing Company, 110 West 34th St., New York City; monthly; 1922 —).

Police '13 – 13': Chicago Police Department. (Police Printing Co., 865 N. Wells St., Chicago; monthly; 1921 —).

Northwest Police Journal: official publication of the North West Association of Sheriffs and Police. (Northwest Police Journal, Inc., 528 Lyon Bldg., Seattle, Wash.; 1926 —).

'2 – 0' Police Journal: official publication of the San Francisco Police Department. (San Francisco).

Police Journal [official]. (St. Louis, Mo.; 1922 —).

The State Trooper [Michigan State Police]. (Detroit, Michigan; monthly; 1919 —).

The Detective: official Journal of the police authorities and sheriffs of the United States. (Chicago; monthly; 1915 —).

D IX 5 — INTERNATIONAL

International Oeffentliche Sicherheit [in German and French]. (Deutschmeisterplatz 3, Vienna; fortnightly).

D IX 6 — MANDATED TERRITORY: PALESTINE.

The Palestine Police Magazine. (Jerusalem; 1933 —).

D X — POLICE ADMINISTRATION REPORTS

[A few administrations do not publish annual reports, but there are the following among Police Reports published in print annually by the heads of various Police Forces within the British Empire. The place of publication is shown in brackets.]

D X 1 — GREAT BRITAIN.

Commissioner of Police of the *Metropolis.* (H.M.S.O.).

H.M. Inspectors of Constabulary, the Counties and Boroughs, *England and Wales.* (H.M.S.O.).

H.M. Inspector of Constabulary for *Scotland.* (H.M.S.O.).

D X 2 — DOMINIONS.

Australia : New South Wales. Police Dept. (Sydney).
South Australia. Commissioner of Police. (Adelaide).
Western Australia. Commissioner of Police. (Perth).

Canada. Commissioner, Royal Canadian Mounted Police. (Ottawa).
Superintendent, Provincial Police, British Columbia. (Victoria).
Commissioner of Police, Nova Scotia. (Halifax).

New Zealand. Commissioner of Police, Dominion of New Zealand. (Wellington).

South Africa. Commissioner, South African Police [in Annual Dept. Report since 1920]. (Pretoria).

D X 3 — INDIA.

Assam. Inspector General of Police. (Shillong).

Bengal. Inspector General of Police. (Calcutta).

Bihar and Orissa. Inspector General of Police. (Patna).

Bombay. Inspector General of Police. (Bombay).

Burma. Inspector General of Police. (Rangoon).

Central Provinces. Inspector General of Police. (Nagpur).

Madras. Inspector General of Police. (Madras).

N.W. Frontier Province. Inspector General of Police. (Peshawar).

Punjab. Inspector General of Police. (Lahore).

City of Bombay. Commissioner of Police. (Bombay).

City of Calcutta. Commissioner of Police. (Calcutta).

D X 4 — COLONIES.

Bahamas. Commandant of Police, Bahamas Colony. (Nassau).

Barbados. Inspector General, Police Force for Colony of Barbados. (Bridgetown).

Ceylon. Inspector General of Police. (Colombo).

Fiji. Inspector General of Police. (Suva).

Gold Coast. Inspector General of Police. (Accra).

Guiana, British. Inspector General of Police. (Georgetown, Demarara).

Hong Kong. Captain Superintendent of Police (Hong Kong).

Jamaica. Inspector General, Jamaica Constabulary. (Kingston).

Kenya. Commissioner of Police, Colony and Protectorate of Kenya. (Nairobi).

Leeward Islands. Chief Inspector, Leeward Islands Police Force. (Antigua, B.W.I.)

Malay Federated States. Commissioner of Police. (Kuala Lumpur).

Malta. Commissioner of Police. (Valetta).

Mauritius. Inspector General of Police. (Port Louis).

Nigeria. Inspector General of Police. (Lagos).

Rhodesia, Southern. Commissioner, British South African Police. (Salisbury).

Sierra Leone. Commissioner of Police. (Freetown).

Straits Settlements. Inspector General of Police. (Singapore).

Trinidad and Tobago. Inspector General of Constabulary. (Port of Spain, Trinidad).

Zanzibar. Commandant of Police. (Zanzibar).

D X 5 — MANDATED TERRITORY.

Palestine. Inspector General, The Palestine Police Force. (Jerusalem).

Tanganyika. Commissioner, Tanganyika Police and Prisons. (Dar-es-Salam).

D XI — EQUIPMENT

Police Uniforms of the World. Major F. Gilbert Blakeslee. (Norwood, Mass., U.S.A.; Plimpton Press, 1934).

Truncheons: their Romance and Reality. [Describes and illustrates police truncheons]. Erland F. Clark. (Herbert Jenkins, 1935).

E. DETECTION
Principles and Methods.

E 1—GENERAL [*See also* E II].

The Detective Faculty. [Illustrated from judicial records]. W. H. BAILEY. (Cincinnati, U.S.A., Clarke, 1886).

Kriminal Taktik : ein handbuch für das untersuchen von Verbrechen. A. WEINGART. (Leipzig, 1904).

Criminal Investigation. DR. HANS G. A. GROSS. Tr. from German by J. and J. C. Adam. (Madras, Higginbotham, 1906 ; London, Specialist Press, 1907 ; 2nd Edn., 1924 ; 3rd Edn., revised by Norman Kendal, Asst. Comr., Metropolitan Police, London, Sweet & Maxwell, 1934).

The Investigating Officer's Manual, Bengal Police. B. A. COLLINS. (Bengal Govt. Press, 1912).

M.O. (Modus Operandi) in Criminal Investigation and Detection. MAJOR L. [later SIR LLEWELYN] W. ATCHERLEY, Chief Constable, West Riding of Yorkshire. (Privately printed for Police Service, 1913 ; 2nd Edn. revised by Lt.-Col. Frank Brook, Wakefield, County Chief Constable's Office, 1932).

The Control of Professional Crime [in India]. G. P. WHALLEY. (Calcutta, Thacker, 1919).

The Detection of Burglary in India. W. A. GAYER, Director General of Police, Hyderabad. (Calcutta, Thacker, 1920).

Aid to the Detection of Professional Crime. B. N. BANDOPADHYAYA. (Calcutta, 1920).

Manuel élémentaire de Police technique. E. GODDEFROY. (Paris, Godde, 1922).

Manuel de technique policière. E. LOCARD. (Paris, Payot, 1922 ; 2nd Edn., 1934).

The Criminal as a Human Being. [Expert discussion on the Art of Detection]. G. S. DOUGHERTY, formerly Chief of Detectives, New York Police Dept. (New York, Appleton, 1924).

Secret intelligence [*i.e.* detective] *service : Concise instruction in modern methods employed in the development of civil and criminal cases by American and foreign secret service operators.* (Chicago, University of Applied Science, 1925).

Great Detectives and their Methods. GEORGE DILNOT. (G. Bles., 1927).

Practical Points for Policemen : Some Hints on Criminal Investigation. RICHARD OGLE. (Hutchinson, 1930 ; 2nd Edn., revised, *Police Review* Pub. Co., 1931).

Crime and its Detection. [British detective practice from various contributors]. ED. W. Teignmouth Shore, 2 Vols. (Gresham Publishing Co., 1931, 1932).

History of the Criminal Investigation Department at Scotland Yard. MARGARET PROTHERO. (Jenkins, 1931).

The Third Degree. [Weakness of police and demoralising methods]. EMMANUEL H. LAVINE [Police reporter, New York]. (Eveleigh, Nash & Grayson, 1931).

The Real Detective [English practice]. GEORGE DILNOT. (G. Bles, 1933).

The Compleat Crook in France. [French methods of criminal investigation]. F. D. GRIERSON. (T. Butterworth, 1933).

Clues and Crime : The Science of Criminal Investigation. HENRY T. F. RHODES. (Murray, 1933).

Secrets of Scotland Yard. [Crime and its detection from the 18th Century to the present day]. EDWIN T. WOODHALL. (John Lane, 1935).

Modern Criminal Investigation. Deputy Chief Insp. O'CONNELL and DR. HARRY SÖDERMAN. (New York, Funk & Wagnalls, 1935). [Has bibliography].

E II—SCIENTIFIC AIDS TO DETECTION

E II 1 — GENERAL.

Manuele di Polizia Scientifica. G. ALONGI. (Milan, 1898).

La police et l'enquête judiciaire scientifique. ALFREDO NICEFERO. (Paris, Libraire Universelle, 1907).

La Police Scientifique. E. GODDEFROY. (Ostende, 1911).

Science and the Criminal. C. A. MITCHELL. (Pitman, 1911).

Manuel de police scientifique (vols et homicides). Preface by M. LOUIS LÉPINE. R. A. REISS. (Lausanne, 1911).

The application of Surveying to Criminal Investigation. MAJOR F. C. HIRST. (Calcutta; Thacker, Spink, 1914).

L'enquête criminelle et les méthodes scientifiques. E. LOCARD. (Paris, E. Flammarion, 1919, 1923, 1929).

Science and the Investigation of Crime. C. A. MITCHELL. (Royal Society of Arts, March 16, 1921).

The Scientific Detective and the Expert Witness. C. A. MITCHELL. (Heffer, Cambridge, 1930). Revised Edn. of ' The Expert Witness and the application of Science and Art to Human Identification, Criminal Investigation, Civil Actions and History.' (Heffer, 1923).

Traité de Criminalistique. E. LOCARD. (Lyon, Desvigne, Vols. 1–2, 1931; Vols. 3–4, 1933).

Some Persons Unknown, being an account of scientific detection, etc. HENRY T. F. RHODES. (Murray, 1931).

Forensic Chemistry and Scientific Criminal Investigation. A. LUCAS. (E. Arnold, 1931).

Plan Drawing for the Police. JAMES D. CAPE. (Pitman, 1932).

Science and the Police Officer. HENRY T. F. RHODES. (*Police Chronicle*, 1934). [Lectures, reproduced from *The Garda Review*, official organ of the Irish Free State Police.]

The Detection of Crime: An introduction to some methods of Scientific aid in Criminal Investigation. Supt. W. M. ELSE and Asst. Chief Constable J. M. GARROW, Derbyshire Constabulary. (*Police Journal*, Philip Allan, 1934).

Death under the Microscope [some cases of Sir Bernard Spilsbury: Crippen, Rouse, Mahon, etc.]. HAROLD DEARDEN. (Hutchinson, 1934).

La Police et Les Méthodes Scientifiques. DR. EDMOND LOCARD. (Paris, Les Editions Rieder, 1934).

E II 2 — HUMAN IDENTIFICATION.

(a) GENERAL.

Personal Identification: methods for the identification of individuals, living or dead. H. H. WILDER and B. WENTWORTH. (Boston, U.S.A., Badger, 1918).

(b) ANTHROPOMETRY.

Identification of Criminal Classes by Anthropometry. A. BERTILLON. (Methuen, London, 1889).

The Illustrated Guide to the Police Portrait System. C. FASSON. (Calcutta, K. P. Mukherji, 1904).

L'oeuvre d'Alphonse Bertillon. E. LOCARD. (Lyon, Ray, 1914).

Strange Crimes. H. ASHTON-WOLFE. (Hurst & Blackett, 1932). [Studies of methods of Bertillon].

(c) PHOTOGRAPHY.

La photographie judiciaire. R. A. REISS. (Paris, Ch. Mendel, 1903).

Kompendium der gerichlichen photographie. WILHELM URBAN. (Leipzig, Vemnisch, 1909).

The Photographic Department of the Liverpool City Police. (*Police Journal*, Vol. II., p. 534 ; Oct., 1929).

The Fluorescence Test : ultra-violet light in scientific criminal investigation. C. T. SYMONS. (*Police Journal*, Vol. III., p. 235 ; April, 1930).

Uses of ultra-violet light in criminal investigation. DR. H. GOODMAN. (*Police Journal*, Vol. IV., p. 225 ; April, 1931).

Fluorescent Analysis in ultra-violet light. DRS. J. A. RADLEY and J. GRANT. (Chapman & Hall, 1933).

Ultra-violet rays in criminal investigation. DR. FRANK W. MARTIN. (*Police Journal*, Vol. VII., p. 431 ; Oct., 1934).

(*d*) FINGER PRINT SYSTEM [DACTYLOSCOPY].

Finger Prints. SIR W. HERSCHEL. (*Nature*, xxiii., p. 23, Nov. 25, 1880).

Finger Prints. FRANCIS GALTON. (Macmillan, 1892).

Classification and Uses of Finger Prints. SIR EDWARD HENRY. (London, Wyman, 1900, 1906, 1913 ; H.M.S.O. 1922 ; 6th Edn., 1928 ; 7th Edn., 1934).

La Dactyloscopie. Identification des récidivistes par les empreintes digitales. E. LOCARD. (Lyon, 1904).

Daktyloskopie. Verwertung von Fingerabdrücken zu Identifizierungszwecken. K. WINDT and R. S. KODICEK. (Vienna, 1904).

L'identification par les empreintes digitales palmaires. A. YVERT. (Paris, 1905).

Finger Print Photography. O. CROMWELL, Bradford City Police. (London, Elliot Stock, 1907).

L'identification des récidivistes. E. LOCARD. (Paris, Maloine, 1909).

Footprints. An aid to the detection of crime for the police and magistracy. G. W. GAYER. (Nagpur, India ; 1909).

History of the Finger Print System. B. LAUFER. (Smithsonian Institute, Annual Report, 1912 ; Washington, U.S.A., 1913).

La preuve par indice dans le procès pénal. PIERRE GARRAUD. (Paris, Larose et Tenin, 1913).

Hints on Finger Prints, with a telegraphic code. RAI SAHIB HEM CHANDRA BOSE. (Calcutta, Thacker, 1916).

Finger Print Instructor [based on the Henry System]. FRED KUHNE, Bureau of Criminal Investigation, Police Dept., City of New York. (New York, Munn, 1916).

The Origin of Finger-Printing. SIR WILLIAM J. HERSCHEL. (Oxford University Press, 1916). [Discovery, 1858 ; demonstration, 1877].

Telegraphic Code for Finger-Print formulae. C. S. COLLINS. *Police Chronicle*, 1921).

A Manual of Practical Dactylography. HENRY FAULDS. (*Police Review* Publishing Co., 1923).

Single Fingerprint System. JOHN A. LARSON. (New York, Appleton, 1924). [Contains good bibliography].

Instructions on the Methods of Taking Finger Prints. Prepared at the Registry of Criminals, New Scotland Yard. (H.M.S.O., 1928).

Single Finger Prints : A New and Practical Method of classifying and filing single Finger Prints and Fragmentary Impressions. CHIEF INSPECTOR H. BATTLEY. (Finger Print Bureau, New Scotland Yard ; H.M.S.O., 1930).

Finger Print Clues. C. S. COLLINS. (H.M.S.O., 1930).

E II 3 — HANDWRITING [*See also* B III 4].

On Forgery, its detection and illustration. D. T. AMES. (San Francisco, Bancroft, 1900).

The Detection of Forgery. A practical Handbook for the use of Bankers, Solicitors, Magistrates' Clerks and all handling suspected documents. DOUGLAS BLACKBURN and CAPTAIN W. CADDELL. (London, Charles & Edwin Layton, 1909).

L'expertise des faux en écritures par altération. GEORGES BÉROUD. (Thèse de medicine, Lyon, 1923).

L'expertise en écriture, ses méthodes récentes. JACQUES DESTABLES. (Thèse, Paris, 1925).

La valeur de la preuve dans l'expertise des écritures. Mlle. MAGGIE GUIRAL. (Thèse, Lyon, 1927).

The Classification and Identification of Handwriting. C. D. LEE and R. A. ABBEY [Police Dept., Berkeley, California]. (New York, Appleton, 1922).

Experiments with Handwriting. ROBERT SAUDEK. (Allen & Unwin, 1928).

Crime in Ink. [Work of David N. Carvalho, American handwriting expert]. C. CARVALHO and B. SPARKES. (Scribner, 1929). [Contains bibliography].

Questioned Documents. ALBERT S. OSBORN. (Sweet & Maxwell, 1929, 1931). [Contains bibliography].

Forged, Anonymous and Suspect Documents. CAPTAIN ARTHUR J. QUIRKE, Handwriting Analyst to the Department of Justice in the Irish Free State. (Routledge, 1930).

Contested Documents and Forgeries. F. BREWSTER, Document Specialist. (Calcutta Book Company, 1933).

Anonymous Letters: a study in Crime and Handwriting. ROBERT SAUDEK. (Methuen, 1934).

E II 4 — FIREARMS AND BALLISTICS.

The Forensic Examination of Firearms and Projectiles. ROBERT CHURCHILL. (*Police Journal*, Vol. II., p. 367 ; July, 1929).

Identification of Firearms and Forensic Ballistics. MAJOR GERALD BURRARD. (H. Jenkins, 1934).

The Firearms Expert in America. ALLEN PENNELL WESTCOTT. (*Police Journal*, Vol. VII., p. 472 ; Oct. 1934).

The Identification of Firearms. JACK D. GUNTHER and CHARLES O. GUNTHER. (New York, John Wiley ; London, Chapman & Hall, 1935).

E II 5 — POLICE DOGS.

War, Police and Watch Dogs. LT.-COL. E. H. RICHARDSON. (Blackwood, 1910).

The use of Police Dogs: a summary. (Journal of the American Institute of Criminal Law & Criminology, Vol. III., p. 123 ; 1912–13).

Police Dogs and their Training. R. ARUNDEL. (London, *Police Review* Publishing Co., 1920, 1924, 1933).

The Police Dog: his selection and training. R. ARUNDEL. (*Police Journal*, Vol. I., p. 423 ; July, 1928).

Dogs as Detectives in South Africa. COLONEL DE VILLIERS. (*Police Journal*, Vol. II., p. 188 ; April, 1929).

Police Dog Training: German Practice. P. L. CECIL-GURNEY. (*Police Journal*, Vol. III., p. 526 ; Oct., 1930).

E II 6 — WIRELESS.

Wireless Telegraphy for police purposes : British Columbia practice. THOMAS W. S. PARSONS. (*Police Journal,* Vol. III., p. 103 ; Jan., 1930).

The Use of Wireless and Telephony for Police Purposes. F. E. ROBINSON. (*Police Journal,* Vol. III., p. 226 ; April, 1930).

The Invisible Arm. Sergt. J. H. HARKER. (*Police Journal,* Vol. IV., p. 590 ; Oct., 1931).

Pursuit by Wireless. CAPT. A. POPKESS, Chief Constable, Nottingham. (*Police Journal,* Vol. VI., p. 31, Jan., 1933, and Vol. VII., p. 147, April, 1934).

E II 7 — FORENSIC MEDICINE.

The Principles and Practice of Medical Jurisprudence. A. S. TAYLOR. 2 Vols. (1865 ; 8th Edn., Ed. S. Smith and W. G. H. Cook ; Churchill, 1928).

A Manual of Medicine Jurisprudence for India ; including an Outline of the History of Crime against the Person in India. DR. NORMAN CHEVERS. (Calcutta, 1870).

Outlines of Medical Jurisprudence for Indian Criminal Courts. I. D. B. GRIBBLE. (Madras, 1885).

Medical jurisprudence, forensic medicine and toxicology. R. A. WITTHAUS and T. C. BECKER. 2nd Edn. (New York, Wood, 1906–11).

Medical Jurisprudence for India. SURGEON-MAJOR I. B. LYON. (Calcutta, 1904, 1914, 1928).

The Diary of a Police Surgeon. DR. GRAHAM GRANT. (C. A. Pearson, 1920).

Forensic Medicine and Toxicology. I. DIXON MANN. 6th Edn. (Griffin, 1922).

Forensic Medicine illustrated by photographs and descriptive cases. HARVEY LITTLEJOHN. (Churchill, 1925).

A Handbook of Medical Jurisprudence and Toxicology. W. A. BREND. (Griffin, 1928).

Methods and Problems of Medical Education (Ninth Series). [Deals with Institutes of Legal Medicine throughout the World, including those at Edinburgh and Glasgow]. (New York, Rockefeller Foundation, 61, Broadway, 1928).

Aids to Forensic Medicine and Toxicology. W. G. A. ROBERTSON. (Baillière, 1929).

Legal Medicine and Toxicology. R. W. WEBSTER. (Philadelphia, 1930).

Forensic Chemistry and Scientific Criminal Investigation. A. LUCAS. (E. Arnold, 1931).

Forensic Medicine. SYDNEY A. SMITH. 3rd Edn. (Churchill, 1931).

A Text Book of Medical Jurisprudence and Toxicology. JOHN GLAISTER, M.D., and JOHN GLAISTER, Junr., M.D. 5th Edn. (Edinburgh ; E. & S. Livingstone, 1931).

Recent Advances in Forensic Medicine. S. SMITH and J. GLAISTER, Junr. (Churchill, 1931).

Laboratory Manual for the Detection of Poisons and Powerful Drugs. DR. WILHELM AUTENRIETH. Tr. by W. H. Warren. 6th Edn. (Churchill, 1931).

The Medico-Legal Necropsy. Ed. Thomas B. Magath. (Convention in June, 1933, of the American Society of Clinical Pathologists, Milwaukee, Wisconsin, U.S.A. ; Baillière, 1934).

E II 8 — PERIODICALS DEALING WITH MEDICO-LEGAL SUBJECTS OR CRIMINOLOGY (*See also* A I 2 and D IX).

(*a*) England.

Transactions of the Medico-Legal Society. [To 1932]. (11, Chandos Street, W.1., London).

Medico-Legal and Criminological Review. (London, Baillière, Tindall & Co., quarterly). [From 1933].

The Howard Journal : a Review of Modern Methods for the prevention and treatment of crime and juvenile delinquency. (Howard League for Penal Reform ; Parliament Mansions, Victoria St., S.W.1).

(*b*) Europe.

Belgium.

Revue de Droit Pénal et de Criminologie et Archives internationales de médicine légale. (55, Rue Ducale, Brussels).

France [*See also* C IV].

Annales de médicine légale, de criminologie et de police scientifique. (J. B. Baillière ; 19, rue Hauteville, Paris).

Etudes Criminologiques : organe de l'Association des élèves et anciens élèves de l'Institut de Criminologie de l'Université de Paris. (Libraire du Recueil Serèy ; 22, rue Soufflot, Paris).

Revue Internationale de Criminalistique : organe officielle de l'Academie Internationale Criminalistique. Ed. Edmond Locard. (Lyon, 36-42, Passage de Hotel Dieu ; Desvigne).

Germany.

Deutsche Zeitschrift für die gesamte gerichtliche Medizin. (Berlin, Julius Springer).

Archiv für Kriminologie. Directeur, Robert Heindl. (Leipzig, Vogel).

Kriminalistische Monatshefte. (Charlottenburg, Berlin ; Bali Verlag Berger & Co. ; monthly).

Italy.

Archivio di antropologia criminale psichiatria e medicina legale. (Turin, Fratelli Bocca ; bi-monthly).

Spain.

Revista española de criminologia y psiquiatria forense. (Madrid, Imprenta de Juan Pueyo, Luna 29).

(*c*) America.

United States.

Journal of the American Institute of Criminal Law and Criminology. (Chicago, Northwestern University Press ; quarterly).

Argentina.

Revista de identificacion y ciencias penales. (Museo Vusetich, La Plata ; bi-monthly).

Revista de criminologia psiquiatria y medicina legal. (Instituto de Criminologia de la Penitenciaria nacional ; Buenos Aires).

Brazil.

Arquivos de Medicina Legal and Identificaçao. (Rio de Janeiro).

E III—MEMOIRS OF DETECTIVE WORK WRITTEN BY POLICE OFFICERS

E III 1 — GREAT BRITAIN AND IRELAND.

(*a*) England and the Metropolis.

Autobiography of an English Detective. C. Waters [pseud., *i.e.* William Russell]. 2 Vols. (London, J. Maxwell, 1863).

A Life's Reminiscences of Scotland Yard. A. Lansdowne, Det.-Insp., C.I.D., Metropolitan Police. (Leadenhall Press, 1885).

Scotland Yard, Past and Present. T. A. Cavanagh. (London, 1893).

Stories from Scotland Yard, as told by Inspector Messer. E. F. RIDEAL. (Routledge, 1894).

Reminiscences of Chief Inspector John George Littlechild. (Leadenhall Press, 1894).

Twenty Years of Detective Life. JEROME CAMINADA. (Manchester, J. Heywood, 1895; 2 Vols., 1901).

At Scotland Yard [guarding Royalty, etc.]. JOHN SWEENY, late Det. Insp. (Grant Richards, 1904).

The Lighter Side of my official life. SIR ROBERT ANDERSON, Asst. Comr., Metropolitan Police, 1888–1901. (Hodder & Stoughton, 1910).

Scotland Yard Experiences. G. H. GREENHAM. (Routledge, 1912).

Recollections of a Detective. ROBERT A. FULLER. (J. Long, 1912).

Days of my Years. SIR MELVILLE MACNAGHTEN, late Chief of the C.I.D., Scotland Yard. (Edward Arnold, 1914).

Queer People [treats of professional criminals]. SIR BASIL THOMSON, Asst. Comr., Metropolitan Police, 1913–19; Director, Special Branch, 1919–21. (Hodder & Stoughton, 1922).

Crooks and Crime. J. KENNETH FERRIER, formerly Det. Insp., Scotland Yard. (Seeley, Service, 1926).

Rogues and others. CHARLES ARROW, ex-Chief Insp., C.I.D., Metropolitan Police. (Duckworth, 1926).

From Kew Observatory to Scotland Yard. Ex-Chief Insp. W. C. GOUGH. (Hurst & Blackett, 1927).

Reminiscences of an ex-Detective. F. CARLIN. (Hutchinson, 1927).

Memoirs of a Plain Detective. TOM DIVALL. (Benn, 1928).

Detective and Secret Service Days. EDWIN T. WOODHALL. (Jarrolds, 1929).

Detective Days: The Record of Forty-two years' service in the Criminal Investigation Dept. FRED P. WENSLEY, Chief Constable, Scotland Yard, 1924–29. (Cassell, 1930).

Episodes and Reflections. SIR WYNDHAM CHILDS, Asst. Comr., 1921-28. (Cassell, 1930).

From Information Received: The reminiscences of Cecil Bishop. (Hutchinson, 1932).

Forty Years of Man-Hunting. Ex-Supt. ARTHUR F. NIEL, late C.I.D., Scotland Yard. (Jarrolds, 1932).

When I was at Scotland Yard. Ex-Chief Inspector JAMES BERRETT. (Sampson Low, 1932).

On Top of the Underworld. Ex-Det. Insp. CHARLES E. LEACH. (Sampson Low, 1933).

Traitors Within [Special Branch experiences]. HERBERT T. FITCH, ex-Det. Insp., Special Branch, Scotland Yard. (Hurst & Blackett, 1933).

Guardians of the Great [Special Branch work]. EDWIN T. WOODHALL. (Blandford Press, 1934).

Lost London [Peter the Painter, Lenin, Steinie Morrison, etc; East End experiences]. Ex-Det. Serg. B. LEESON. (Stanley Paul, 1934).

Savage of Scotland Yard. [Murderers, spies, burglars, pickpockets and tricksters]. Ex-Supt. PERCY SAVAGE. (Hutchinson, 1934).

Secrets of Scotland Yard. E. T. WOODHALL. (Falcon Series; John Lane, 1935).

Cornish of the 'Yard.' His reminiscences [33 years] *and cases.* [Includes twelve murder cases]. Ex-Supt. G. W. CORNISH. (John Lane, 1935).

Crime within the Square Mile. [34 years with the City of London Police]. Ex-Chief Det. Insp. ERNEST NICHOLLS. (John Long, 1935).

(*b*) SCOTLAND.

Curiosities of Crime in Edinburgh during the last thirty years. J. McLEVY. (Edinburgh, W. P. Nimmo, 1861).

Recollections of a Glasgow Detective Officer. T. P. McNAUGHT. (London, Simpkin, 1887).

Experiences of a City Detective. JAMES McGOVAN. (Glasgow, Menzies, 1889).

Clues or Leaves from a Chief Constable's Note Book. W. HENDERSON, Chief Constable, Edinburgh. (Edinburgh, Oliphant, Anderson & Ferrier, 1889).

Adventures of a Detective. A. CARMICHAEL. (Simpkin, 1892).

Personal Adventures of a Detective. A. CARMICHAEL. (Glasgow, Morrison Bros., 1900).

Tracking Glasgow Criminals. W. ELLIOTT, Ex-Insp. (Glasgow, Press Pub. Co., 1904).

(*c*) IRELAND.

Twenty-five years in the Secret Service: Recollections of a spy. [Fenian conspiracies]. MAJOR HENRI LE CARON. (Heinemann, 1893).

Irish Conspiracies: Recollections of John Mallon. F. M. BUSSY. (London, Everett, 1910).

E III 2 — BRITISH EMPIRE.

AFRICA, SOUTH.

Secret Service in South Africa. D. BLACKBURN and W. CADDELL. (Cassell, 1911).

AFRICA, WEST.

A Gold Coast Detective. SIR J. T. HUTCHINSON. (*Africa Society*, Vol. XVII., p. 227; 1918).

Momo and I. FRANK HIVES. [District Commissioner and his orderly in Nigeria, 1910–1914]. (John Lane, 1934).

AUSTRALIA.

The Detectives' Album: Tales of the Australian Police. W.W. (Melbourne, 1871).

CANADA.

Memoirs of a Great Detective. Incidents in the Life of John Wilson Murray, late Supt. C.I.D., Toronto, Canada. Ed. Victor Spear. (Heinemann, 1904; New York, Baker, 1905; Toronto, Revell, 1905).

INDIA.

Detective Experiences in Bengal. (*Calcutta Review*, Vol. LXXX., 1885).

Revelations of an Indian Detective. R. REID, Supt. Calcutta Detective Dept. (Calcutta, City Press, 1885).

Some Records of Crime: Diary of an officer of the Thuggee and Dacoitie Police, 1866–1867. GEN. CHAS. HERVEY. 2 Vols. (Sampson Low, 1892).

Reminiscences of an Indian Police Official [Bombay Presidency]. T. C. ARTHUR [pseud., *i.e.* A. T. CRAWFORD]. (Sampson Low, 1894; Roxburghe Press, 1898).

Romantic Episodes of a Brilliant Detective. R. REID. (Calcutta, City Press, 1899).

Reminiscences of a Bengal Detective. N. BONNERJEE. (Calcutta, 1900).

Police and Crime in India [Bombay Presidency]. SIR EDMUND COX. (Stanley Paul, 1911).

Life in the Indian Police [Bengal Presidency]. C. E. GOULDSBURY. (Chapman & Hall, 1912).

MALAYA.

A Yellow Sleuth. NOR NALLA, Det. Serg., Federated Malay States Police. (Hutchinson, 1931).

E III 3 — EUROPE.

FRANCE.

Memoirs de Joseph Fouché, duc d'Otrante, Ministre de la Police générale. (Paris, 1824).

Memoirs jusqu'en 1827. E. F. VIDOCQ. (Paris, 1828–29).

Autobiography of a French Detective from 1818 to 1858. M. CANLER, ancien Chef du service de Sûreté. (London, 1863). [Tr. by Sir C. F. Lascelles-Wraxall of the French Edition which was suppressed by the French Govt.].

La Police Parisienne. GUSTAVE MACÉ. (Charpentier, 5 Vols., 1885–89 ; Eugène Fasquet, Paris, 2 Vols., 1897–1904).

My First Crime. G. MACÉ, Chief of the Paris Detective Police. (London, Vizetelly, 1886).

The World of Crime. M. F. GORON, Chief of Detective Staff, Paris. (Hurst & Blackett, 1907).

Memoirs of Claude, Chef de la Police de Sûreté under the Second Empire. Tr. by Katherine P. Wormeley. (Constable, 1908).

My Royal Clients. XAVIER PAOLI. Tr. by A. Teixera de Mattos. (Hodder & Stoughton, 1911).

Mes Souvenirs. LOUIS LÉPINE. (Paris, Payot, 1929).

Indiscretions of a Prefect of Police : Anecdotes of Napoleon and the Bourbons from the papers of Count Réal. Ed. Arthur L. Hayward. (Cassell, 1929).

Dramas of French Crime : Being the Exploits of a Celebrated Detective. RENÉ CASSELLARI. (Hutchinson, 1930).

The Underworld of Paris : Secrets of the Sûreté. ALFRED MORAIN, Prefect of Police. (Jarrolds, 1930).

The French Police from within. RENÉ FARALICQ [in charge Special Brigade, Paris, 1919-25]. (Cassell, 1933).

ITALY

Memorie di un Questore. A. BONDI. (Milan, La Grande Attualita, 1900). Dillingham, 1907).

E III 4 — AMERICA (*See also* A III 3 and B IV 3).

History of the United States Secret Service [Bureau of the National Detective Police]. GENERAL L. C. BAKER. (Philadelphia, 1868).

Knots Untied : or ways and by-ways in the hidden life of American detectives. G. S. McWATTERS. (Hartford, Burr, 1871).

Memoirs of the United States Secret Service [Detective work]. GEORGE P. BURNHAM. (Boston, Lee, 1872).

Thirty Years' Battle with Crime : or the crying shame of New York, as seen under the broad glare of an old detective's lantern. J. H. WARREN. (Poughkeepsie, White, 1874). [Gamblers and swindlers included].

Three years with Counterfeiters, etc. GEORGE P. BURNHAM. (Boston, 1875).

Detectives of Europe and America : or Life in the Secret Service. A selection of celebrated cases of the most renowned detectives. G. S. McWATTERS. (Hartford, 1877 ; Chicago, Laird, 1892).

Strikers, Communists, Tramps and Detectives. A. PINKERTON. (New York, Carleton, 1878, 1882, 1884).

The Gypsies and the Detectives. A. PINKERTON. (New York, Carleton, 1879; Dillingham, 1907).

Criminal Reminiscences. A. PINKERTON. (New York, Carleton, 1879).

The Molly Maguires and the Detectives. A. PINKERTON. (New York, Carleton, 1880).

Recollections of a New York Chief of Police. GEORGE W. WALLING. (Denver, 1890).

Professional Thieves and the Detectives. A. PINKERTON. (New York, Dillingham, 1890, 1908).

Our Rival: the Rascal . . . . the conflict between the criminals . . . and . . . . the Police. BENJ. P. ELDENRIDGE, Supt. of Police, and WILLIAM B. WATTS, Ch. Insp., Detective Bureau, Boston. (Boston, Pemberton, 1897).

Notes of an Itinerant Policeman. J. A. FLYNT. (Boston, 1900).

Hands up: in the world of Crime, or 12 years a detective. CLIFTON R. WOOLDRIDGE. (Chicago, Charles C. Thompson Co., 1906).

The Masked War: the story of a peril that threatened the United States by the man who uncovered the dynamite conspirators and sent them to jail. WILLIAM J. BURNS. (Hodder & Stoughton, 1914).

The Adventures of the Secret Service [Anti-sabotage methods of American Army in France]. MAJOR C. E. RUSSELL. (New York; Doubleday, Page, 1923).

The Man they Couldn't Escape: adventures of Detective Michael Fraschetti, Commanding officer, Italian Squad, New York City Police Dept. Narrated to P. BURANELLI. (Selwyn & Blount, 1930).

On the Track of Murder. ARTHUR CAREY, late Deputy Chief of the Homicide Bureau, New York City Police Dept. (Jarrolds, 1930).

Behind the Green Lights [describes gangsterism]. CAPT. CORNELIUS M. WILLEMSE [in collaboration with GEORGE J. LEMNER and JACK KOFOEK]. (New York, Knopf, 1931; John Long, 1933).

Ten Thousand Public Enemies. COURTNEY R. COOPER. [Describes the Division of Investigation of the Federal Dept. of Justice, U.S.A.]. (Boston, Little; London, Lovat Dickson, 1935).

E IV—DETECTIVE LITERATURE BY WRITERS OTHER THAN POLICE OFFICERS

E IV 1 — GENERAL.

The Revelations of a Private Detective. A. FORRESTER. (Ward, Lock, 1883).

Scotland Yard Detective Stories. (London, General Publishing Co., 1888).

Shadows of Life: series of true detective stories. CHARLES MEYER. (London, 1895).

Some Clever Detective Feats. G. R. SIMS. (*Strand Magazine*, June, 1914–Dec., 1914).

Memories of a Private Detective. HERBERT MARSHALL. (Hutchinson, 1925).

Scotland Yard. JOSEPH GOLLOMB. (Hutchinson, 1926). [Comparative methods of London, Paris, Berlin and Vienna].

Before Scotland Yard: classic tales of Roguery and Detection. Collected and arranged by PETER HAWORTH. (Oxford, Blackwell, 1927).

From Clue to Dock. C. McCLUER STEVENS. (Stanley Paul, 1927).

The Man Hunters [Comparative studies]. MELVILLE DAVISSON POST [American writer]. (Hutchinson, 1927).

Great Detectives and their Methods. G. DILNOT. (G. Bles, 1927).

Triumphs of Detection: a Book about Detectives. G. DILNOT. (G. Bles, 1928).

Unusual Detective Stories: adventures of a chemist. F. A. FAWKES. (Harrison, 1930).

Strange Company. S. T. FELSTEAD. (Hutchinson, 1930).

Triumphs of Detection: stories of crime. H. L. ADAM. (Collins, 1931).

100 Mysteries for armchair detectives : based on actual crimes and mysteries investigated at Scotland Yard. JOHN C. CANNELL. (John Long, 1932).

The Real Detective. G. DILNOT. (G. Bles, 1933).

Clues and Crime. HENRY T. F. RHODES. (Murray, 1933).

Famous Feats of Detection and Deduction. [11 cases, English, Canadian, American, French ; refers to Macé, Goron, Vidocq, Berré, Carlin, Prothero, Berrett, Murray, Belshaw, Heinrich, Pinkerton]. LEONARD R. GRIBBLE. (Harrap, 1933).

E IV 2 — FRANCE.

The Invisible Web. Strange Tales of the Sûreté. H. ASHTON-WOLFE. (Hurst & Blackett, 1928).

The Forgotten Clue : Tales and Methods of the Sûreté. H. ASHTON-WOLFE. (Hurst & Blackett, 1929, 1930).

Strange Crimes, culled from the archives of the Paris Sûreté. H. ASHTON-WOLFE. (Hurst & Blackett, 1932).

E IV 3 — AMERICA.

Famous Detective Mysteries. G. BARTON. (Philadelphia, 1926).

Dramatic Crimes. A study in mystery and detection. M. MACKAYE. (Garden City, New York, 1928).

Strange and Mysterious Crimes [24 true detective stories]. (New York, Macfadden Publications, 1929).

Masterstrokes of Crime Detection. L. WREN. (Garden City, New York, 1929).

The Pinkertons : a Detective Dynasty [Allan, Robert, William]. RICHARD WILMER ROWAN. (Hurst & Blackett, 1931).

F. CRIMINAL TRIALS

F I—COLLECTIONS [*See also* B I].

Celebrated Trials and Remarkable Cases of Criminal Jurisprudence from the earliest times to the year 1825. GEORGE BORROW. 6 Vols. (London, Knight & Lacey, 1825). Revised by E. H. Bierstadt. (J. Cape, 1928).

Cobbett's Complete Collection of State Trials. From A.D. 1163. 10 Vols. Ed. William Cobbett. Continuation from A.D. 1680. 33 Vols. Ed. T. B. and T. J. Howell. (London, 1809–1828).
New Series from A.D. 1820 to 1858. Ed. Sir John Macdonell and J. E. P. Wallis. (London, 1888–1898).

Criminal Trials. 2 Vols. (London, Charles Knight, 1832–35).

English Causes Celèbres: a report of Remarkable Trials. GEORGE L. CRAIK. (London, Knight, 1844).

Narratives of Remarkable Criminal Trials. P. J. VON FEUERBACH. Tr. by Lady Duff-Gordon. (London, Murray, 1846).

Modern State Trials [A.D. 1820–1850]. 2 Vols. W. C. TOWNSEND. (Longmans, 1850).

The Romance of the Forum: Narratives, Scenes and Anecdotes from Courts of Justice. PETER BURKE. 4 Vols. (London, 1852).

Narratives from Criminal Trials in Scotland. JOHN HILL BURTON. 2 Vols. (Chapman & Hall, 1852).

Criminal Celebrities: a Collection of Memorable Trials. L. WRAXALL. (London, Kent, 1861).

Remarkable Convictions. By a Writer to the Signet. (Edinburgh, Nimmo, 1865).

Remarkable Trials of all Countries [U.S.A., Great Britain, Ireland, France]. T. DUNPHY and T. J. CUMMINS. (New York, Diossy, 1870).

Remarkable Trials and Notorious Characters [from Half-hanged Smith, 1709, to Oxford, 1840]. [Illustrated by Phiz]. CAPT. L. BENSON. (London, 1871).

A Collection of Reports of Celebrated Trials, civil and criminal. W. O. WOODALL. (London, Shaw, 1873).

State Criminal Trials. 2 Vols. (London, Charles Knight, 1882).

Famous Trials of the Century [Weare and Thurtell, and 7 other trials]. J. B. ATLAY. (Grant Richards, 1899).

State Trials: Political and Social. H. (later SIR HARRY) L. STEPHEN. (Duckworth, 2 Vols., 1899; Second Series, 2 Vols., 1902).

Memories of Famous Trials. EVELYN BURNABY. (London, Sisley's, 1907).

Romantic Trials of Three Centuries. HUGH CHILDERS. (John Lane, 1913).

Twelve Scots Trials [A.D. 1570–1889). WILLIAM ROUGHEAD. (Edinburgh, Green, 1913).

Famous Irish Trials. M. MCDONNELL BODKIN. (Dublin, Maunsel, 1918).

Famous Judges and Famous Trials. CHARLES KINGSTON. (Stanley Paul, 1923).

Famous Poison Trials. H. EATON. (Collins, 1923).

Dramatic Days at the Old Bailey. C. KINGSTON. (Stanley Paul, 1923).

The Drama of the Law. JUDGE E. (later SIR EDWARD) PARRY. (Fisher Unwin, 1924).

Murder, Piracy and Treason: a Selection of Notable English Trials. R. POSTGATE. (J. Cape, 1925).

Famous Trials Retold. Some society Causes celèbres. H. WYNDHAM. (Hutchinson, 1925).

Famous Trials of History [Mary Queen of Scots, Col. Blood, Warren Hastings, Capt. Kidd, Eugene Aram]. EARL OF BIRKENHEAD. (Hutchinson, 1926).

Some Famous Medical Trials. L. A. PARRY. (Churchill, 1927).

More Famous Trials [Marie Antoinette, Charles Peace, etc]. EARL OF BIRKENHEAD. (Hutchinson, 1928).

Curious Trials and Criminal Cases from Socrates to Scopes. EDWARD HALL BIERSTADT. (Hutchinson, 1929).

Witch Hunting and the Witch Trials [A.D. 1559–1736]. C. L'ESTRANGE EWEN. (Routledge, 1929).

Dramas of the Dock: True Stories of Crime. [Murder trials of the 19th Century]. GUY B. H. LOGAN. (Stanley Paul, 1930).

Thou shalt do no Murder [sketches of famous murder trials]. ARTHUR LAMBTON. (Hurst & Blackett, 1930).

The Tragic Brides and other famous Murder Trials. H. L. ADAM. (Collins, 1930).

Echoes of Causes Celèbres. ARTHUR LAMBTON. (Hurst & Blackett, 1931).

What is your Verdict? WM. ROUGHEAD. (Faber & Faber, 1931, 1933).

Notable Trials: Difficult Cases [A. G. Macrae and five other cases]. R. STORRY DEANS. (Chapman & Hall, 1932).

Murders and Murder Trials: 1812–1912. H. M. WALBROOK. (Constable, 1932).

Six Trials [Wallace case; Harold Greenwood, etc.]. WINIFRED DUKE. (Gollancz, 1934).

F II—PUBLISHERS' SERIES

F II 1 — NOTABLE BRITISH TRIALS SERIES (William Hodge & Co., Edinburgh and London).

[Criminal cases arranged in the chronological order of the actual cases. The date in parenthesis is the date of publication].

A.D.

1605 *Trial of Guy Fawkes.* Ed. Donald Carswell. (1934).

1685 *Bloody Assizes.* Ed. J. G. Muddiman. (1929).

1701 *Trial of Captain Kidd.* Ed. Graham Brooks. (1930).

1724 *Jack Sheppard.* Ed. Horace Bleackley and S. M. Ellis. (1933).

1736 *Trial of Captain Porteous.* Ed. W. Roughead. (1909).

1752 *Trial of Mary Blandy.* Ed. W. Roughead. (1914).

1752 *Trial of James Stewart: The Appin Murder.* Ed. David W. Mackay. (1907).

1759 *Eugene Aram: his Life and Trial.* Ed. Eric R. Watson. (1913).

1765 *Trial of Katherine Nairn.* Ed. W. Roughead. (1926).

1788 *Trial of Deacon Brodie.* Ed. W. Roughead. (1906).

1792 *Bounty Mutineers.* Ed. Owen Rutter. (1931).

1817 *Trial of Abraham Thornton.* Ed. Sir John Hall, Bart. (1926). [Forgery Cases].

1824 *Trial of Henry Fauntleroy.* Ed. Horace Bleackley. (1924).

A.D.

1824 *Trial of Thurtell and Hunt.* Ed. Eric R. Watson. (1921).

1828 *Burke and Hare.* Ed. W. Roughead. (1921).

1849 *James Blomfield Rush.* Ed. W. Teignmouth Shore. (1928).

1856 *Trial of William Palmer.* Ed. George H. Knott. (1912). [*See also* 'The Times' Report of the Trial of William Palmer, London, 1856; and B II 1].

1857 *Trial of Madeleine Smith.* Ed. F. Tennyson Jesse. (1921). [Earlier Edition by A. Duncan Smith, 1905].

1859 *Trial of Dr. Smethurst.* Ed. Leonard A. Parry. (1931).

1862 *Trial of Jessie McLachlan.* Ed. W. Roughead. (1926).

1864 *Trial of Franz Muller.* Ed. H. B. Irving. (1911).

1865 *Trial of Dr. Pritchard.* Ed. W. Roughead. (1906).

1875 *Trial of the Wainwrights.* Ed. H. B. Irving and Sir Edward Marshall Hall. (1920).

1877 *Trial of the Stauntons: The Penge Mystery.* Ed. J. B. Atlay. (1911).

1878 *Trial of Eugène Marie Chantrelle.* Ed. A. Duncan Smith. (1928). [*Also* Sweet & Maxwell, 1906].

1879 *Trial of Kate Webster.* Ed. Elliott O'Donnell. (1925).

1879 *Trial of the City of Glasgow Bank Directors.* Ed. William Wallace. (1905).

1879 *Trials of Charles Frederick Peace.* Ed. W. Teignmouth Shore. (1926). *See also* under B II 1.

1882 *Trial of George Henry Lawson.* Ed. Hargrave L. Adam. (1913).

1886 *Trial of Adelaide Bartlett.* Ed. Sir John Hall, Bart. (1927).

1889 *Trial of Mrs. Maybrick.* Ed. H. B. Irving. (1912).

1889 *Trial of John Watson Laurie.* [The Arran Murder]. Ed. W. Roughead. (1932).

1892 *Trial of Thomas Neill Cream.* Ed. W. Teignmouth Shore. (1923).

1893 *Trial of Alfred John Monson.* Ed. John W. More. (1908).

1903 *Trial of George Chapman* [Severin Klosowski]. Ed. H. L. Adam. (1930).

1903 *Trial of Samuel Herbert Dougal.* [Moat Farm Murder]. Ed. F. Tennyson Jesse. (1928).

1903 *Trial of William Gardiner* [second trial of Peasenhall case]. Ed. William Henderson. (1935).

1877–1904 *Adolf Beck.* Ed. Eric R. Watson. (1924).

1909–1928 *Trial of Oscar Slater.* Ed. W. Roughead. (Original case, 1910).

1910 *Trial of Hawley Harvey Crippin.* Ed. Filson Young. (1920).

1910 *Trial of John Alexander Dickman.* Ed. S. O. Rowan-Hamilton. (1914).

1911 *Trial of Steinie Morrison.* Ed. Hon. H. Fletcher Moulton. (1922).

1912 *Trial of the Seddons.* Ed. Filson Young. (1914).

1915 *Trial of George Joseph Smith.* Ed. Eric R. Watson. (1922).

1916 *Trial of Sir Roger Casement.* Ed. George H. Knott. (1917).

1920 *Trial of Harold Greenwood.* Ed. Winifred Duke. (1931).

1922 *Trial of Ronald True.* Ed. Donald Carswell. (1925).

1922 *Trial of Frederick Bywaters and Edith Thompson.* Ed. Filson Young. (1923).

A.D.

1922 *Trial of H. R. Armstrong.* Ed. Filson Young. (1927).

1924 *Trial of Jean Pierre Vaquier.* Ed. R. H. Blundell and R. E. Seaton. (1929).

1927 *Trial of John Donald Merrett.* Ed. W. Roughead. (1929).

1927–1928 *Trial of F. G. Browne and W. H. Kennedy.* Ed. W. Teignmouth Shore. (1930).

1928 *Trial of Benjamin Knowles.* Ed. Albert Lieck. (1933).

1930 *Trial of Sidney Harry Fox* [Margate hotel crime]. Ed. F. Tennyson Jesse. (1934).

1931 *Trial of Alfred Arthur Rouse* [Blazing car murder]. Ed. Helena Normanton. (1931).

1931 *The Royal Mail Case* [Lord Kylsant]. Ed. Collin Brooks. (1933).

F II 2 — THE FAMOUS TRIALS SERIES (London, G. Bles).

[Criminal cases, arranged in the chronological order of the actual cases. The date in parenthesis is the date of publication].

A.D.

1827 *The Murder of Maria Marten.* (1928). [Reprint of a contemporary account by J. Curtis, published by Kelly, London, 1828].

1849 *The Trial of Professor Webster* [murder of Dr. George Parkman]. G. DILNOT. (1928).

1857 *Jim the Penman* [James Townsend Saward]. G. DILNOT. (1930). *See also* B II 1.

1860 *The Case of Constance Kent* [Road Hill murder]. JOHN RHODE. (1928). [Case of Inspector Whicher].

1873 *The Bank of England Forgery* [George and Austin Bidwell]. G. DILNOT. (1929).

1877 *The Trial of the Detectives* [Chief Inspectors Druscovitch, Palmer and Clarke, and Inspector Meiklejohn]. G. DILNOT. (1928).

1882 *The Peltzer Case* [Murder of Guillaume Bernays]. GERARD HARRY. (1928).

1901 *The Trial of Herbert John Bennett* [Yarmouth Beach murder], with introd. by EDGAR WALLACE. (1929).

1906–1915 *The Thaw Case.* F. A. MACKENZIE. (1928).

1919 *Landru.* F. A. MACKENZIE. (1928).

1922 *The Trial of Thomas Henry Allaway* [Bournemouth murder]. W. LLOYD WOODLAND. (1929).

1923 *The Trial of Alexander Campbell Mason.* HON. H. FLETCHER MOULTON. (1930).

1924 *The Trial of Patrick Mahon.* EDGAR WALLACE. (1928).

1925 *The Trial of Norman Thorne* [Crowborough Chicken Farm murder]. MRS. HELENA NORMANTON. (1929).

1930 *The Trial of William Henry Podmore.* HON. H. FLETCHER MOULTON and W. LLOYD WOODLAND. (1931).

1931 *The Trial of Alfred Arthur Rouse* [Blazing car murder]. SYDNEY TREMAYNE. (1931).

F III—SOME INDIVIDUAL STUDIES

Trial of Gangram and Shew Prasad [the Shoes murder]. Ed. Arthur Page. (Calcutta, Thacker, 1927).

Trial of the Twins. JOHN WINSFORD. (Cassell, 1928).

The Case of Jean Calas [1761]. F. H. MAUGHAM. (Heinemann, 1928). *See also L'Affaire Calas.* MARC CHASSAIGNE. (Paris, Perrin, 1929). Tr. by Raglan Somerset. (Hutchinson, 1930).

The Trial of Count Königsmarck [Murder of Thomas Thynne in the 17th Century]. HON. EVELINE GODLEY. (Peter Davies, 1929).

French Justice: seven months under sentence of death [France and Guiana]. MANUEL MENENDEZ VALDES. Tr. by Dora Round. (Faber & Faber, 1930).

The Sacco-Vanzetti Case [seven years between sentence and execution]. OSMUND K. FRAENKEL. (Routledge, 1931).

The Monster of Dusseldorf [1930]. MARGARET SEATON WAGNER. (Faber & Faber, 1932).

The Trial of William Herbert Wallace. Ed. W. F. Wyndham-Brown. (Gollancz, 1933).

F IV—REGIONAL LITERATURE

AFRICAN, SOUTH, TRIALS.

Famous South African Trials. N. DEVITT. (Pretoria, 1930).

Up for Murder [trials in South Africa]. B. BENNETT and F. P. ROUSSEAU. (Hutchinson, 1933).

AMERICAN TRIALS.

American Criminal Trials. P. W. CHANDLER. 2 Vols. (Boston; Little, Brown, 1841–44; London, A. Maxwell).

Celebrated Trials. HENRY L. CLINTON. (New York, Harper, 1897).

American Criminal Reports. Digest of Cases and Notes contained in Vols. I.–XV. of American Criminal Reports. (Chicago, Callaghan, 1910).

The Crime and Trial of Leopold and Loeb. M. MCKERNAN. (Allen & Unwin, 1925).

American State Trials [collection of criminal trials]. Ed. J. D. Lawson. (St. Louis, Thomas, 1914–1926).

The Milligan Case. Ed. Samuel Klaus. (Notable American Trials Series; Routledge & Kegan Paul, 1929).

The Molineux Case [Poisoning of Mrs. Adams]. Ed. Samuel Klaus. (Notable American Trials Series; Routledge & Kegan Paul, 1929).

The New World of Crime: Famous American Trials [12 cases]. EPHESIAN [*i.e.* C. E. BECHHOFER ROBERTS]. (Eyre & Spottiswoode, 1933). [Introductory essay on the reading of Criminal Trials, by Robert Burrows, K.C.].

AUSTRALIAN TRIALS.

Famous Australian Trials. Trial of R. G. Griggs [1928]. (Sweet & Maxwell, 1930).

BELGIAN TRIALS.

Les Causes Celèbres de Belgique. PAUL DARRAS. (Paris, A. Savine, 1888).

FRENCH TRIALS.

Judicial Dramas: or the romance of the French Criminal Law. HENRY SPICER. (Tinsley, 1872).

Causes Criminelles et mondaines de — [from 1880 to 1897]. ALBERT BATAILLE. (19 Vols.; Paris, E. Dentu, 1881 to 1898).

Les grand procès de l'histoire. HENRI-ROBERT. (8 Vols.; Paris, Payot, 1922–1932).

GERMAN TRIALS.

Der Neue Pitaval [Collections of Criminal Cases]. J. C. HITZIG and W. HÄRING. (Leipzig, Brockhaus, 1842–1890).

Der Pitaval der Gegenwart. R. FRANK, G. ROSCHER and H. SCHMIDT. (Tübingen, Mohr, 1907–1914).

Behind the Scenes of German Justice [mostly political trials]. *Reminiscences of a Barrister, 1882–1933.* ALFRED APFEL. (John Lane, 1935).

F V—GENERAL REFERENCES TO TRIALS

Leaves of a Life: being the reminiscences of Montagu Williams, Q.C. (Macmillan, 1890).

Memories of Famous Trials. EVELYN BURNABY [constant attendant at trials]. (London, Sisley's, 1907).

Prisoners at the Bar: sidelights on the Administration of Criminal Justice. ARTHUR TRAIN. (Scribners, 1906, 1908).

Reminiscences of Sir Henry Hawkins, Baron Brampton. Ed. Richard Harris. (Nelson, 1918).

Famous Judges and Famous Trials. C. KINGSTON. (Stanley Paul, 1923).

In Court and out of Court: some personal recollections. E. BOWEN-ROWLANDS. (Hutchinson, 1925).

The Judges and the Judged. C. KINGSTON. (John Lane, 1926).

Forty Years at the Criminal Bar: reminiscences and impressions. E. D. PURCELL. (Fisher Unwin, 1926).

Fourteen English Judges. EARL OF BIRKENHEAD. (Cassell, 1926).

Sir Richard Muir: a Memoir of a Public Prosecutor. S. T. FELSTEAD. Ed. by Lady Muir. (John Lane, 1927).

Lord Darling and his Famous Trials. EVELYN GRAHAM [pseud.]. (Hutchinson, 1929).

Life of Sir Edward Marshall Hall. EDWARD MARJORIBANKS. (Gollancz, 1929).

Fifty Years of Famous Judges. EVELYN GRAHAM [pseud.]. (Long, 1931).

Convicting the Innocent: errors of Criminal Justice [65 cases, chiefly American]. EDWIN M. BORCHARD and E. RUSSELL LUTZ. (Publications of Institute of Human Relations; Newhaven, Yale Univ. Press; Oxford Univ. Press, 1932).

Judicial Wisdom: or Famous Cases of Mr. Justice McCardie. Ed. Albert Crew. (Nicholson & Watson, 1933).

Recollections. SIR HENRY DICKENS. (Heinemann, 1934).

The Trials of Mr. Justice Avory. BERNARD O'DONNELL. (Rich & Cowan, 1935).

F VI—CRIMINAL LAW AND PROCEDURE [*See also* F IV & D II].

F VI 1 — ENGLAND AND WALES. *See also* D II 1.

General View of the Criminal Law of England [includes accounts of seven notable criminal trials]. JAMES [later SIR JAMES] FITZJAMES STEPHEN. (Macmillan, 1863).

History of the Criminal Law of England. SIR JAMES F. STEPHEN. 3 Vols. (Macmillan, 1883).

Observations on the growth of criminal law in ancient communities. RICHARD R. CHERRY, Lord Chief Justice of Ireland. (Macmillan, 1890).

The Police Code: general Manual of the Criminal Law. SIR HOWARD VINCENT. (1881, 1893; Butterworth, 17th Edn. 1931).

The Criminal Law: a sketch of its principles and practice. HENRY W. DISNEY and HAROLD GUNDRY. (Stevens, 1895; 2nd Edn. Ed. Albert Lieck, 1926).

The Poor Prisoners' Defence Act, 1903 [3 Edw. 7, chap. 38]. THOMAS R. BRIDGWATER. (Butterworth, 1904).

The Administration of Justice in Criminal Matters in England and Wales. G. GLOVER ALEXANDER. (Cambridge University Press, 1911, 1915).

Observations on English Criminal Law and procedure. JOHN W. JEUDWINE. (King, 1920).

The Justice at Work. ALBERT LIECK. (Butterworth, 1922).

[Sir William Oldnall] *Russell on Crimes: a treatise on crimes and misdemeanours.* 8th Edn. Ed. R. E. Ross and G. B. McClure. (Sweet & Maxwell, 1923).

Three Criminal Law Reformers—Beccaria, Bentham, Romilly. COLEMAN PHILLIPSON. (Dent, 1923; New York, Dutton, 1923).

Justice and the Poor in England. F. C. G. GURNEY-CHAMPION. (Routledge, 1926).

[Sir James Fitzjames] *Stephens' Digest of the Criminal Law.* Ed. Sir Herbert Stephen and Sir Harry Stephen. 7th Edn. (Sweet & Maxwell, 1926).

Criminal Procedure: an outline of the criminal process in this country. GORDON C. TOUCHE and FREDERIC E. RUEGG. (Stevens, 1926; 2nd Edn. 1933).

The Criminal Justice Acts. A. LIECK and A. C. L. MORRISON. (Stevens, 1927).

[Sir John] *Jervis on Coroners: a practical treatise on their office and duties.* 7th Edn. Ed. F. D. Jones. (Sweet & Maxwell, 1927).

Historical Trials. SIR JOHN MACDONELL. Ed. Prof. R. W. Lee. (Clarendon Press, 1927). [Contains comparison of legal procedure in trials of Socrates, Joan of Arc, Galileo, Mary Queen of Scots, Sir W. Raleigh, etc.].

The Law of Coroners. T. ODAWAY. (Butterworth, 1927).

[Henry] *Roscoe's Digest of the Law of Evidence and the Practice in Criminal Cases.* 15th Edn. Ed. Anthony Hawke. (Sweet & Maxwell, 1928).

Outlines of Criminal Law. C. S. KENNY. 13th Edn. (Cambridge University Press, 1929).

A Magistrates' Handbook. S. R. C. BOSANQUET and D. H. J. CHALMERS. (Benn, 1929).

English Courts of Law. W. BLAKE ODGERS. (Sweet & Maxwell, 1930).

In quest of Justice [on the need for reform in the English judicial system]. CLAUD MULLINS. (Murray, 1931).

Criminal Justice in England: a Study in Law Administration from an American point of view. PROF. PENDLETON HOWARD. (Macmillan, 1931).

Evidence in Criminal Cases. W. SHAW. 2nd Edn. (Butterworth, 1932).

Criminal Appeal Reports, 1908–1931. HERMAN COHEN. (Sweet & Maxwell, 1932).

Magisterial Law. ALBERT and SOPHIE LIECK. (Pitman, 1933).

Principles and Practice of the Criminal Law. S. F. HARRIS. 15th Edn. Ed. A. M. Wilshere. (Sweet & Maxwell, 1933).

Criminal Law and Procedure in a Nutshell. MARSTON GARSIA. 5th Edn. (Sweet & Maxwell, 1934).

[John Frederick] *Archbold's Pleading, Evidence and Practice in Criminal Cases.* 29th Edn. Ed. R. E. Ross and T. R. F. Butler. (Stevens; Sweet & Maxwell, 1934).

Police Law: An arrangement of Law and Regulations for the use of Police Officers. C. C. H. Moriarty, Asst. Chief Constable, Birmingham. (Butterworth, 1929, 1931; revised 4th Edn., 1935).

[Albert] *Gibson's Criminal and Magisterial Law, 1890.* Arthur Weldon and L. C. Warmington. 10th Edn. (*Law Notes* Pub. Co., 1934).

[John] *Stone's Justices' Manual.* Ed. F. B. Dingle, solicitor, Sheffield. (Shaw; Butterworth; 67th Edn., 1935).

F VI 2 — SCOTLAND.

Criminal Procedure and the Law of Evidence in Scotland. John Morren. (Edinburgh, Hodge, 1928).

A Practical Treatise on the Criminal Law of Scotland. Lord Kingsburgh. (Edinburgh, 1929).

F VI 3 — FRANCE.

A History of Continental Legal Procedure, with special reference to France. A. Esmain. Tr. by John Simpson. (London, Continental Legal History Series, Vol. V., 1913).

Traité théorique et pratique de Droit Pénal Français. R. Garraud. 5 Vols. (Paris, 1913–24).

French Justice. Manuel Menendez Valdes. Tr. by Dora Round. (Faber, 1930).

Courts and Judges in France, Germany and England. R. C. K. Ensor. (Oxford Univ. Press, 1933).

F VI 4 — RUSSIA.

Soviet Administration of Criminal Law. J. Zelitch. (Law School Series, Pennsylvania Univ. Press; Oxford Univ. Press, 1932).

Penal Code of the Russian Socialist Federal Soviet Republic, up to Dec. 1933. British Foreign Office. (H.M.S.O., 1934).

F VI 5 — AMERICA.

[Joel P.] *Bishop on Criminal Law.* 9th Edn. Ed. John M. Zane and Carl Zollmann. (Chicago, Flood, 1923).

Crime and Criminal Law in the United States. Harry Best. (New York, Macmillan, 1930). [Contains bibliography].

Criminal Justice in America. [Culver Lectures of 1924]. Roscoe Pound. (New York, 1930).

F VII—COURTS

F VII 1 — OLD BAILEY.

The Old Bailey and Newgate. Charles Gordon [*pseud., i.e.,* John Ashton]. (Unwin, 1902).

The Central Criminal Court: a Survey of the History of the Court, Newgate, the Fleet and other Jails. (Eyre & Spottiswoode, 1909).

Dramatic Days at the Old Bailey. C. Kingston. (Stanley Paul, 1923).

The Old Bailey: History, Constitution, Functions and Notable Trials [daily routine and procedure]. Albert Crew. (Ivor Nicholson & Watson, 1933).

Life and Death at the Old Bailey. R. Thurston Hopkins. (H. Jenkins, 1934).

The History of Newgate and the Old Bailey. W. Eden Cooper. (Underwood Press 1935).

F VII 2 — POLICE COURTS [*See also* H 1].

Mornings at Bow Street. J. WRIGHT, Reporter. (London, Wheatley, 1825). [Contains illustrations by George Cruikshank].

Ten Years a Police Court Judge. JUDGE WIGLITTLE [pseud. *i.e.*, A. A. PUTNAM]. New York, Funk, 1884).

Chronicles of Bow Street Police Office; with an account of the Magistrates, Runners and Police. P. H. FITZGERALD. 2 Vols. (Chapman & Hall, 1888).

The Paris Police Courts. GERALD P. MORIARTY. (New York, Scribner, 1894).

The Prisoner in the Dock: my four years' experience in the London Police Courts. J. GREENWOOD. (Chatto & Windus, 1902).

Pictures and Problems from London Police Courts. THOMAS HOLMES [Police Court Missionary]. (E. Arnold, 1900, 1902, 1908).

Snowden's Magistrates' Assistant and Police Officers' Guide. 11th Edn. (Butterworth, 1905).

The London Police Court: To-day and To-morrow. HUGH R. P. GAMON. (Dent 1907).

The Whirlpool: scenes from the Toronto Police Court. H. M. WODSON. (Toronto, 1917).

The Recollections of a Police Magistrate. COL. GEORGE T. DENISON. (Toronto, Canada; Museum Book Co., 1920).

Police Court Practice and Procedure in New Zealand. F. W. SHORTLAND. (Auckland, N.Z., 1921).

The Justice at Work. ALBERT LIECK [Chief Clerk, Bow Street Police Court]. (Butterworth, 1922).

When Mercy Seasons Justice: a short history of the Church of England in the Police Courts. H. H. AYSCOUGH. (C.E.T.S., 1923).

The Loom of the Law: experiences and reflections of a Metropolitan Police Magistrate. J. A. R. CAIRNS. (Hutchinson, 1922, 1924).

Thirty Years at Bow Street Police Court. W. T. EWENS. (Werner Laurie, 1924).

The Police Court and its Work. HENRY T. WADDY, Magistrate, Thames Police Court. (Butterworth, 1925).

Tales told to the Magistrate. R. E. CORDER [pseud.]. (Melrose, 1925).

The Poor Man's Court of Justice; 25 years as a Metropolitan Magistrate. CECIL CHAPMAN. (Hodder & Stoughton, 1925).

Box and the Dock. JOHN GORDON SHERLOCK. (Fisher Unwin, 1926).

Justice and the Poor in England. F. G. GURNEY-CHAMPION. (Routledge, 1926).

Inasmuch: the Story of the Police Court Mission, 1876–1926. J. HASLOCK POTTER. (Williams & Norgate, 1927).

Justice and the Police in England. ALBERT LIECK. (Butterworth, 1928, 1929).

The Life of a London Beak. H. L. CANCELLOR, late Magistrate, Marylebone, Thames and Marlborough Police Courts. (Hurst & Blackett, 1930).

The Police Court Missionary's Story. H. COURTENAY ORCHARD. (Walsall, Staffs., Christian Workers' Armoury, 1931).

The History of the Bow Street Runners. G. ARMITAGE. (Wishart, 1932).

From the Bench [Reflections on Courts of Justice and Magisterial Administration]. CECIL CHAPMAN. (Hodder & Stoughton, 1932).

Henry Fielding, Novelist and Magistrate [Bow Street and Westminster Magistrate, 1748]. B. M. JONES. (Allen & Unwin, 1933).

English Justice. 'SOLICITOR.' (Routledge, 1934). [Attack on the English Police Courts].

Memories of a Magistrate, including Twenty-five years on the South African Bench. NAPIER DEVITT (late first Criminal Magistrate, Johannesburg). (London, H.F. & G. Witherby, 1934).

Laughter in Court [Police Courts]. DUDLEY BARKER. (Methuen, 1935).

F VII 3 — JUVENILE COURTS. [*See also* A V and H I].

Juvenile Court Laws in the United States. Ed. Hastings H. Hart. (Russell Sage Foundation; New York, Charities Pub. Committee, 1910).

Juvenile Court and the Community. THOMAS D. ELLIOT. (New York, Macmillan, 1914).

Juvenile Courts and Probation. BERNARD FLAXNER and ROGER H. BALDWIN. (New York, Century Co., 1914; Richards, 1915).

Six Years in a Juvenile Court. W. B. WALLACE. (Montreal, *McGill University Magazine*, Vol. XVI., p. 362; 1917).

Children's Courts. W. [later SIR WILLIAM] CLARKE HALL, Metropolitan Magistrate and President, Shoreditch Children's Court. (Allen & Unwin, 1926).

Juvenile Courts in the United States. HERBERT H. LOW. (Oxford Univ. Press, 1927).

The Dangerous Life [work of the founder of Denver Juvenile Court]. BEN B. LINDSEY and RUBE BROUGH. (London, Harold Shaylor, 1931).

Organisation of Juvenile Courts and the results obtained hitherto. (League of Nations Advisory Commission for the Probation and Welfare of Children and Young People, Child Welfare Committee; 1931, iv., 13; Geneva, 1932).

The Law Relating to Children and Young Persons. SIR WILLIAM CLARKE HALL and A. C. L. MORRISON. (Butterworth, 1934).

G. PENOLOGY

G I—PRINCIPLES AND METHODS OF PUNISHMENT

G I 1 — GENERAL. [*See also* G IV].

Essay on Crimes and Punishments [Trattato dei Delitti e delle Pene. Cesare Bonesana, Marchese di BECCARIA (1735–1793)]. (Monaco, 1764; Tr. in most European languages; first Tr. in English 1769). *Crimes and Punishments* [contains the best English Tr. of Beccaria]. J. A. FARRER. (Chatto & Windus, 1880).

Crimes and Punishments in Ireland. E. HAYES. 2 Vols. (Dublin, 1842).

On Punishment and Prisons. OSCAR, Crown Prince of Sweden. Tr. by A. May, from Swedish. (Smith, Elder, 1842).

Principles of Penal Law. Part I.—Political Remedies for the evil of offences. Part II.—Rationale of Punishment. Part III.—Indirect methods for preventing crimes. JEREMY BENTHAM. [Included in *Works of Jeremy Bentham*]. Ed. John Bowring. (Edinburgh, Tait, 1843).

The Advantages of a separate system of Imprisonment. REV. J. FIELD. 2 Vols. (London, 1846).

A System of Penal Discipline, with a report on the treatment of prisoners in Great Britain and Van Diemen's Land. HENRY P. FRY. (Longmans, 1850).

Punishment and Prevention as to Criminals. ALEX THOMSON [of Banchory]. (Nisbet, 1857).

Report on the Select Committee on the present state of discipline in Gaols and Houses of Correction. (H.M.S.O., 1863).

Humanity and Humanitarianism, with reference to prison systems of Great Britain and the United States, the question of lunacy and capital punishment. WILLIAM TALLACK. (London, Kitto, 1871).

Reformatory Prison Discipline, as developed by the Rt. Hon. Sir Walter Crofton in the Irish Convict Prisons. MARY CARPENTER. (Longmans, 1872).

Prisons and Reformatories at Home and Abroad [International Penitentiary Congress, 1872]. Ed. Edwin Pears. (Longmans, 1872).

Outline of Penology. J. R. CHANDLER. (Philadelphia, 1875).

Principles of Punishment, as applied to the administration of the Criminal Law. Serjeant E. W. COX. (London, Law Times Office, 1877).

The Gaol Cradle: who rocks it? REV. B. WAUGH. (Isbister, 1880).

The Punishment and Prevention of Crime. COL. SIR EDMUND F. DUCANE, Surveyor-General of Prisons. (Macmillan, 1885).

Criminalité et Répression. ADOLPHE POVIS, Inspector-General of Belgian Prisons. (Brussels, 1885).

The State and the Prison. R. VAUX. (Philadelphia, 1886).

Penological and Preventive Principles: with special reference to Europe and America, and to Crime, Pauperism and their Prevention. W. TALLACK. (London, Wertheimer, 1889, 1896).

The Prison Question. CHAS. H. REEVE. (Chicago, Knight & Lennard, 1890).

Old-Time Punishments. WILLIAM ANDREWS. (Simpkin, Marshall, 1890).

The Prison : a dialogue. HENRY B. BREWSTER. (Williams, 1890).

La Crime et la peine. LOUIS PROAL. (Paris, Felix Alcan, 1892, 1914).

Punishment and Reformation : an Historical sketch of the rise of the Penitentiary System. DR. F. H. WINES, U.S.A. Agent for Census on Crime, Pauperism and Benevolence. (New York, Thomas Crowell, 1895 ; London, Sonnenschein, 1895 ; revised Edn. by W. B. Lane, 1919).

Curious Punishments of Bygone Days. MRS. A. M. EARLE. (Chicago, Stone, 1896).

The Individualisation of Punishment. RAYMOND SALEILLES. (Paris, 1898 ; Tr. by R. S. Jastrow, Modern Criminal Science Series ; Boston, Little, 1911 ; Heinemann, 1911).

The Science of Penology : the Defence of Society against Crime. H. M. BOIES. (New York, Putnam, 1901).

Recent Object Lessons in Penal Science. A. R. WHITEWAY. (Sonnenschein, 1st Series, 1898 ; 2nd Series, 1900 ; 3rd Series, 1902).

Traité de Science et de Législation pénitentiaires. P. CUCHE. (Paris, 1905).

Prisons, Police and Punishment : an enquiry into the census and treatment of Crime and Criminals. EDWARD CARPENTER. (London, A. C. Fifield, 1905, 1907).

Strafe und Verbrechen, Geschichte und Organisation des Gefängniswesens. P. POLLITZ. (Leipzig, B. G. Teubner, 1910).

Criminal responsibility and social restraint. ROY MADDING McCONNELL. (New York, Scribner, 1912 ; Murray, 1912).

The Modern Prison Curriculum : a General Review of our Penal System. Dr. R. F. QUINTON, of Holloway Prison. (Macmillan, 1912).

Penal Philosophy. GABRIEL TARDE. (Paris, 1892, 1900, 1903 ; Tr. by Rapelje Howell ; Modern Criminal Science Series, Heinemann, 1913).

Wards of the State : an official view of Prison and the Prisoner. TIGHE HOPKINS. (Herbert & Daniel, 1913).

On Punishment : a modern view of the rational treatment of crime. CARL HEATH. (G. Bell & Sons, 1913).

The Rationale of Punishment. HEINRICH OPPENHEIMER. (Univ. of London Press, 1913).

A History of Penal Methods : Criminals, Witches, Lunatics. GEORGE IVES. (Stanley Paul, 1914).

Our Prison System. ALEC COOK. (London, Drane's Danegeld House, 1914).

The Flogging Craze : a statement of the case against corporal punishment. HENRY S. SALT. (Allen & Unwin, 1916).

Prisons as Crime Factories. A. FENNER BROCKWAY. (International Bookshops, 1919).

Penal Discipline. Dr. MARY GORDON, H.M.I. Prisons. (Routledge, 1922).

Penology an educational problem. H. H. HART. (New York, Russell Sage Foundation, 1923). [Contains references on penology].

Prison Reform at Home and Abroad : a short history of the International movement since the London Congress of 1872. SIR EVELYN RUGGLES-BRISE [1857-1935]. (Macmillan, 1924).

Curing the Criminal : a Treatise on the Philosophy and Practice of Modern Correctional Methods. JESSE O. STUTSMAN. (New York, Macmillan, 1926).

The Repression of Crime : studies in Historical Penology. H. ELMER BARNES. (New York, Doran, 1926 ; Allen & Unwin, 1926).

Criminology and Penology. PROF. JOHN LEWIS GILLIN, University of Wisconsin. (Jonathan Cape, 1927).

The Morality of Punishment, with some suggestions for a general theory of ethics. A. C. EWING. (Kegan Paul, 1929).

Taming the Criminal: Adventures in Penology. J. L. GILLIN. (New York, Macmillan, 1931).

Conflicting Penal Theories in statutory Criminal Law. MABEL ELLIOTT. (Chicago University Press; Cambridge University Press, 1931).

The Crime of Punishment [as deterrent]. MARGARET WILSON. (Jonathan Cape, 1931).

Bygone Punishments. WILLIAM ANDREWS. (1899; 2nd Edn., P. Allan, 1931).

What we put in Prisons and in preventive and rescue homes. DR. G. W. PAILTHORPE. (Williams & Norgate, 1932). [Crime and aberrant behaviour; psychology of lawmakers as well as of lawbreakers].

From Punishment to Prevention. PROSANTO KUMAR SEN. (Oxford University Press, 1932). [Contains bibliography].

Martyrdom in our Times: an introductory Essay on Prison and Punishment. A. MITCHELL INNES. (Williams & Norgate, 1932).

Report from the Departmental Committee on the Employment of Prisoners. (H.M.S.O., 1933).

The Lawbreaker: a critical study of the Modern Treatment of Crime. E. ROY CALVERT and THEODORA CALVERT. (Routledge, 1933).

Prisons and a Changing Civilisation. DR. M. HAMBLIN SMITH. (Twentieth Century Library; John Lane, 1934). [Describes the emotionally unbalanced, the morally eccentric and the congenitally perverse].

Penal Institutions. THORSTEN SELLIN. Art. in *The Encyclopaedia of the Social Sciences*, Vol. XII. (Macmillan, 1934). [Contains bibliography].

Recent changes in Prison Administration. G. D. TURNER, Asst. Prison Commissioner. (*Police Journal*, Vol. VII., p. 36; Jan., 1934).

G I 2 — CAPITAL PUNISHMENT.

Facts relating to the Punishment of Death in the Metropolis. EDWARD G. WAKEFIELD. (London, 1832).

Capital Punishment [Die Todesstrafe, etc.]. PROF. C. J. A. VON MITTERMAIER. Ed. J. M. Moir. (Heidelberg, 1862; London, Smith, Elder, 1865).

The Death Penalty: a consideration of the objections to Capital Punishment. ANDREW J. PALM. (Putnam, 1891).

The Penalty of Death, or the Problem of Capital Punishment. JOSIAH OLDFIELD. (Bell, 1901).

Select list of references on Capital Punishment. HERMAN MEYER. (Washington, U.S.A.; Government Printing Office, 1912; Supplement, 1924).

Capital Punishment in the United States. RAYMOND T. BYE. (Philadelphia; Committee of Friends, 1919). [Has bibliography].

The Judgment of Death. E. BOWEN-ROWLANDS. (Collins, 1924).

Man's Judgment of Death: Analysis of the operation and effect of Capital Punishment, based on Facts, not on Sentiment. LEWIS E. LAWES, Warden of Sing-Sing Prison. (New York, Putnam, 1924).

Selected articles on Capital Punishment. Ed. Lamar T. Beman. (New York; H. W. Wilson, 1925). [Has bibliography].

Capital Punishment. CLIFFORD KIRKPATRICK. (Philadelphia, 1925).

Capital Punishment in the 20th Century. E. ROY CALVERT. (Putnam, 1927).

A Handbook on Hanging. CHARLES DUFF. (Cayme Press, 1928).

The Hangmen of England. "Jack Ketch" through the centuries. HORACE BLEACKLEY. (Chapman & Hall, 1929).

Report from the Select Committee on Capital Punishment. (*British Parliamentary Papers,* 1930–31, Vol. VI.; H.M.S.O., 1931).

A History of Capital Punishment, with special reference to Capital Punishment in Great Britain. JOHN LAURENCE. (Sampson Low, 1932). [Contains bibliography].

Pamphlets of National Council for the Abolition of the Death Penalty. (Parliament Mansions, Orchard Street, London, S.W.1).

G I 3 — TRANSPORTATION. [*See* also G III 2—India].

Remarks on Transportation. RICHARD WHATELY, Archbishop of Dublin. (London, B. Fellowes, 1834).

Defence of Transportation in reply to the Archbishop of Dublin. In his second letter to Earl Grey. COL. GEORGE (later SIR GEORGE) ARTHUR. (London, G. Cowie, 1835).

Transportation and Colonization. J. D. LANG, D.D. (London, A. J. Valpy, 1837).

The Felonry of New South Wales: being a faithful picture of the real romance of life in Botany Bay. JAMES MUDIE. (Smith & Elder, 1837).

Thoughts on Convict Management and other subjects connected with the Australian Penal Colonies. CAPT. MACONOCHIE, R.N. (Hobart, 1838).

The Convict Ship and England's Exiles. Dr. C. A. BROWNING, R.N. (London; Hamilton, Adams, 1847).

Convict Life in New South Wales and Van Diemen's Land. C. WHITE. (Bathurst, 1889).

Old Convict Days. L. BECKE. (London, Unwin, 1899).

Governor Arthur's Convict System. Van Diemen's Land, 1824–1836. A Study in Colonization. WILLIAM DOUGLAS FORSYTH. (Imperial Studies Committee of the Royal Empire Society; Longmans, 1935).

G II—REFORM OF PENAL SYSTEMS

John Howard and the Prison World of Europe [1726–1790]. W. H. DIXON. (Jackson, 1850).

Silvio Pellico [1788–1854]. MARCHESA GIULIA FALLETTI. (Bentley, 1866).

John Howard. E. C. S. GIBSON. (Methuen, 1901).

Elizabeth Fry [1780–1845]. G. K. LEWIS. (Headley Bros., 1910).

The Prisoners' Friends: John Howard, Elizabeth Fry and Sarah Martin. CONSTANCE WAKEFORD. (Headley Bros., 1917).

Prison Reform at Home and Abroad. SIR E. RUGGLES-BRISE. (Macmillan, 1925).

John Howard, Prison Reformer. JOHN G. ROWE. (London, Epworth Press, 1927).

Dom Jean Mabillon. A Prison Reformer of the 17th Century. T. SELLIN. (*Journal of the American Institute of Criminal Law and Criminology,* Vol. XVII., p. 581; 1926–27).

G III—PENAL INSTITUTIONS

G III 1 — GENERAL ACCOUNTS OF PRISONS. [*See also* G III 2].

The State of the Prisons in England and Wales with Preliminary Observations and an account of some Foreign Prisons and Hospitals. JOHN HOWARD. (Warrington; 1st Edn., 1777; 4th Edn., Ed. John Aikin, 1792. Abridged under title *The State of the Prisons,* Ed. Kenneth Ruck; Everyman's Library, Dent, 1929).

Account of the Principal Lazarettos in Europe. JOHN HOWARD. (Warrington, 1789). Extracts included in *The State of the Prisons,* Ed. Kenneth Ruck. (Dent, 1929).

State of the Prisons in England, Scotland and Wales. J. NEILD. (London, 1812).

Facts and Observations in relation to extension of State Prisons in England, also bearing on Poverty and Crime. J. BUCHANAN. (New York, 1834).

Le Système pénitentiare en Europe et aux Etats Unis. C. LUCAS. 3 Vols. (Paris, 1836–38).

Rapport sur les Prisons de l'Angleterre, de l'Ecosse, de la Hollande, de la Belgique, et de la Suisse. L. MOREAU. (Paris, Cristophe, 1838).

Revelations of Prison Life with an enquiry into Prison Discipline and Secondary Punishments. G. L. CHESTERTON. (Hurst & Blackett, 1856, 1857).

Prisons and Reformatories at Home and Abroad. [International Penitentiary Congress, 1872]. Ed. Edwin Pears. (London, Longmans, 1872).

The State of Prisons and Child-saving Institutions in the Civilized World. E. C. WINES. (Cambridge, Mass., U.S.A.; J. Wilson, 1880).

John Howard's Winter Journey, 1773–74. Ed. W. A. Guy. (London, De la Rue & Co., 1882).

The Prisons of the World: Crimes, Criminals and Convicts. CHARLES COOK [Evangelist]. (London, Morgan & Scott, 1891, 1892).

Secrets of the Prison House, or Gaol Studies and Sketches including some account of foreign penal systems. MAJOR A. GRIFFITHS. 2 Vols. (Chapman & Hall, 1894).

Report from the Departmental Committee on Prisons. (H.M.S.O., 1895).

Modern Prison Systems: their organization and regulation in various countries of Europe and America. C. R. HENDERSON. (Washington, U.S.A.; Government Printing Office, 1903).

The Prison Breakers: a Book of Escapes from Captivity [John Nevison, Jack Sheppard, Louis Cartouche, Louis Napoleon, Frederic Trenck, etc.]. ALBAN M. PHILIP. (Philip Allan, 1927).

Elizabeth Fry's Journey on the Continent, 1840–41; from the diary kept by her niece Elizabeth Gurney. Ed. R. Brimley Johnson. (Lane, 1931).

The Modern English Prison. L. W. FOX, Secretary, Prison Commission. (Routledge & Kegan Paul, 1934). [Contains bibliography of relevant official literature]

G III 2 — REGIONAL LITERATURE.

(a) GREAT BRITAIN AND IRELAND. [*See also* G IV and G V].

ENGLAND.

The London Prisons: with a description of the chief provincial prisons. W. HEPWORTH DIXON. (London, Jackson & Walford, 1850). [Refers to the Tower, the Hulks, Pentonville, Newgate, Coldbath Fields, Reading Gaol, etc.].

Results of the system of separate confinement administered at Pentonville Prison. JOHN T. BURT. (Longmans, 1852).

The Criminal Prisons of London and Scenes of Prison Life. HENRY MAYHEW and JOHN BINNY. (Griffin, Bohn, 1862).

Reports and Observations on the discipline and management of Convict Prisons. SIR JOSHUA JEBB. (London, 1863).

Memorials of Millbank and Chapters in Prison History. MAJOR ARTHUR GRIFFITHS. (Chapman & Hall, 1875, 1884).

The Chronicles of Newgate. MAJOR A. GRIFFITHS. 2 Vols. (Chapman & Hall, 1884, 1894, 1895, 1896).

The Old Bailey and Newgate. CHARLES GORDON [pseud.]. (Fisher Unwin, 1902).

The Story of Dartmoor Prison. BASIL [later SIR BASIL] THOMSON. (Heinemann, 1907).

Our Prisons. ALEXANDER PATERSON. (Hugh Rees, 1910).

The English Convict. Dr. CHARLES GORING. (Wyman, 1913).

The English Prison System. SIR EVELYN RUGGLES-BRISE, Chairman, Prison Commission. (Macmillan, 1921). [Advocated judicious classification of criminals and other reforms].

English Prisons under Local Government [Vol. VI. of 'English Local Government']. SIDNEY WEBB [later LORD PASSFIELD] and BEATRICE WEBB. (Longmans, 1922).

English Prisons of To-day: being the Report of the [unofficial] Prison System Enquiry Committee of the Labour Research Department. Ed. Stephen Hobhouse and A. Fenner Brockway. (Longmans, 1922).

The English Penal System. G. THOMAS. (*Contemporary Review*, August, 1922).

The Convict of To-day: an authorised investigation of our prisons to-day. SYDNEY A. MOSELEY. (Cecil Palmer, 1927).

Life in London's Great Prisons. [Wormwood Scrubs and Wandsworth]. T. WHYTE MOUNTAIN. (Methuen, 1930).

London Prisons of to-day and yesterday: plain facts and coloured impressions. ALBERT CREW. [Bibliography of 22 items]. (Nicholson & Watson, 1933).

Dartmoor Prison: 1806–1932. A. J. RHODES. (J. Lane, 1933).

The Modern English Prison. L. W. FOX, Secretary, Prison Commission. (Routledge, Kegan Paul, 1934). [Contains bibliography of relevant official literature].

SCOTLAND.

Notes on a visit made to some of the prisons in Scotland and the North of England with Elizabeth Fry [in 1818]. JOSEPH JOHN GURNEY. (London, Constable, 1819; Norwich, Josiah Fletcher, 1847).

Report of the Prisons Department in Scotland. (H.M.S.O.; annual).

IRELAND.

Report addressed to the Marquess of Wellesley, Lord Lieutenant of Ireland. Sec. I. on the Prisons in Ireland. ELIZABETH FRY and JOSEPH JOHN GURNEY. (Norwich, Josiah Fletcher, 1847).

The Purgatory of Prisons, or an Intermediate stage between the Prison and the Public [new Irish system]. REV. ORBY SHIPLEY. (Oxford, Parker, 1857).

The Irish Convict System, more especially the intermediate Prison. FRANZ VON HOLTZENDORFF. Translated. (Dublin, 1860).

Observations on the Treatment of Convicts in Ireland. By Four Visiting Justices of the West Riding Prison in Yorkshire. (Simpkin, Marshall, 1862).

Report on English and Irish Prisons. MAJOR J. JACKSON. (London, 1904).

Report of General Prisons Board, Irish Free State. (Dublin, annual).

(*b*) BRITISH EMPIRE.

AUSTRALASIA.

Thoughts on Convict Management, and the subjects connected with the Australian Penal Colonies. CAPT. MACONOCHIE, R.N. (Hobart, 1838).

Convict System in Australia. ERIC GIBB. (Fisher Unwin, 1899).

Old Convict Days [Tasmania]. LOUIS BECKE. (Fisher Unwin, 1899).

Sidelights on Convict Life [New Caledonia]. GEO. C. GRIFFITH. (Long, 1903).

CANADA.

Canada's Greatest Prison. W. J. McLEOD. (*Canadian Magazine*, Vol. VI., p. 1, 1895).

Canadian Penal Institutions. CORAL W. TOPPING. (Social Service Monographs ; Chicago, U.S.A., University of Chicago Press, 1930 ; Canada, Toronto, 1929 ; Vancouver, 1934).

INDIA.

Notes on Jails and Jail Discipline in India, 1867–68. A. P. HOWELL. (Calcutta, Home Department Selection LXXII., 1869).

Prison Labour as an Instrument of Punishment, profit or reformation : an episode in the prison history of Lower Bengal. DR. F. J. MOUAT. (*Journal of the Society of Arts*, Feb. 23, 1872).

Report on the Indian Jail Conference [President, W. B. Jones]. (Calcutta, Home Secretariat Press, 1877).

Report on the Jail Committee of Surgeon-Major Lethbridge and Dr. Walker. (Calcutta, Superintendent Government Printing, 1888–89).

Report of the Prisons Conference of 1892. [President, A. (later Sir Alfred) S. Lethbridge]. (Calcutta, Superintendent Government Printing, 1892).

The Juvenile Jail at Bareilly. MITHAN LAL. (Allahabad; United Provinces Government Press, 1911).

Control of Crime in India [describes the Indian Penal System]. Dr. C. R. HENDERSON. (Chicago, *Journal of the Institute of Criminal Law and Criminology*, Sept. 1913).

Report of the Indian Jail Committee [President, Sir A. Cardew] *1919–1920.* (H.M.S.O.; Cmd. 1303 ; 1921).

Crime and Punishment in Ancient India. RAMOPRASAD DAS GUPTA. (Kegan Paul, 1930).

Imprisonment and Detention in India. LT.-COL. W. G. HAMILTON. (*Asiatic Review*, Vol. XXVI., p. 421, ; July, 1930).

STRAITS SETTLEMENTS.

Prisoners their own Warders : Record of the convict prison at Singapore [1825–1873], Bencoolen, Penang and Malacca. MAJOR J. F. McNAIR. (Constable, 1899).

(*c*) EUROPE.

AUSTRIA

The Jail . . . . . experiences in 1916 [A Czech in an Austrian prison]. J. S. MACHAR Tr. by P. Selver. (Oxford, Blackwell, 1921).

BELGIUM.

Du Côté de l'ombre. Carnets d'un médecin de prison. L. DELATTRE. (Bruxelles, 1925).

Notice sur l'organisation des établissements pénitentiaires. MINISTÈRE DE LA JUSTICE, Belgium. (Louvain, 1929).

CZECHO-SLOVAKIA.

The Prison System in the Czecho-Slovakian Republic. MINISTERSTVO SPRAVEDLNOSTI. (Prague, 1930).

FRANCE.

The Bastille, its History and Chronicles. CAPT. THE HON. D. BINGHAM. (Chapman & Hall, 1888).

Les Prisons de Paris et les Prisonniers. ADOLPHE GUILLOT. (Paris, E. Dentu, 1890).

Les Prisons de Mont Saint-Michel [1425–1864]. ETIENNE DUPONT. (Paris, Perrin, 1913).

Les Prisons [Prison system of France]. ARMAND MOSSE. (Paris, E. de Boccard, 1926, 1929).

Condemned to Devil's Island: the biography of an unknown convict. BLAIR NILES. (London, J. Cape, 1928).

French Justice: seven months under sentence of death. MANUEL MENENDEZ VALDES. Tr. by Dora Round. (Faber & Faber, 1930).

The Grim Bastille. F. M. KIRCHEISEN. (Hutchinson, 1930).

The Horrors of Cayenne: the experiences of a German as a French bagno-convict. B. HEIM. (Constable, 1930).

Devil's Island [in Guiana]. W. E. ALLISON-BOOTH. (Putnam, 1931).

GERMANY.

Handbuch des Gefängniswesens. FRANZ VON HOLTZENDORFF and E. VON JÄGEMANN. (Hamburg, 1877, 1888).

Deutches Gefängniswesen. E. BUMKE. (Berlin, 1928).

Crime and Punishment in Germany. THEODOR HAMPE. Tr. by M. Letts. (Routledge, 1929).

ITALY

Le nostre carceri e i nostri riformatorii. G. CURLI and A. BIANCHI. (Milan, 1902).

RUSSIA.

Buried Alive, or Ten Years of Penal Servitude in Siberia. F. DOSTOZEFFSKY. (Longmans, 1881).

In Russian and French Prisons. PRINCE PETER KROPOTKIN. (Ward & Downey, 1887).

Siberia and the Exile System. G. KENNAN. 2 Vols. (New York, Century Co., 1891).

Prison Russia. MAURICE GEHRI. (Saint Blaise, Foyer Solidariste, 1909).

Letters from Russian Prisons. (C. W. Daniel, 1926).

My Twenty-six Prisons and my Escape from Solovetski. YOURI D. BEZSONOV. (Cape, 1929).

In the Clutches of the Tcheka [includes Russian prisons and convict settlements]. BORIS CEDERHOLM. Tr. by F. H. Lyon. (Allen & Unwin, 1929).

Soviet Russia fights Crime. LENKA VON KOERBER. (Routledge, 1934). [Study of prison system by eight years' resident].

SPAIN.

Estudios Penitenciarios. Las Prisiones de Londres y las nuestras. F. CABRERIZO. (Madrid, 1911).

Evolución penitenciaria en España. R. SALLILAS [1885–1923]. 2 Vols. (Madrid, 1919).

Instituciones Penitenciarias y similares en España. F. CADALSO. (Madrid, 1922).

SWITZERLAND.

Schweizerische Gefängniskunde. E. HAFNER and E. ZÜRCHER. (Berne, 1925).

(*d*) AFRICA–EGYPT.

Recollections and Reflections. COLES PASHA, late Inspector-General of Prisons, Egypt. (London, St. Catherine's Press, 1919).

(e) AMERICA: UNITED STATES.

On the Penitentiary system in the United States and its application to France. G. DE BEAUMONT and ALEXIS DE TOCQUEVILLE. (Paris, Fournier, 1833). Tr. by Francis Lieber. (Philadelphia, Carey, 1833; Brussels, 1837).

Report on the Penitentiaries of the United States, addressed to H.M. Principal Secy. of State for the Home Dept. (*with 18 plans of various State Prisons*). W. CRAWFORD. (London, 1834, 1835).

Secrets of the American Bastille. W. H. WINDER. (Philadelphia, 1863).

Report on the Prisons and Reformatories of the United States and Canada. E. C. WINES and T. W. DWIGHT. (Albany, New York State; Van Benthuysen, 1867).

Physical and Industrial Training of Criminals [Monographs of the Industrial Training of Criminals]. HAMILTON D. WEY. (New York, 1888).

The Problem of Cain: a study in the treatment of criminals. W. TRUMBULL. (Newhaven, U.S.A., Tuttle, 1890; London, 1890).

The American Siberia [Florida]. J. C. POWELL [14 years in southern convict camp]. (Chicago; H. J. Smith, 1891).

Prison Systems in the United States [Reports prepared for the International Prison Commission]. S. J. BARROWS. (U.S. House Document, 566, 56th Congress, 1st Session; Washington, Govt. Printing Offices, 1900).

Life in Sing Sing. Number 1500. (Indianapolis, Bobbs, 1904).

My Life in Prison [San Quentin Prison, California]. DONALD LOWRIE. (New York, Kennerley, 1912; John Lane, 1912).

Within Prison Walls [voluntary confinement at State prison at Auburn, New York]. T. MOTT OSBORNE. (New York, Appleton, 1915).

Society and Prisons. T. MOTT OSBORNE. (Newhaven, Yale University, 1916; H. Milford, 1916). [Yale Lectures on Responsibility of Citizenship].

A Modern purgatory [Tombs prison, New York]. C. DE FORNARO. (New York, Kennerley, 1917).

The Prison and the Prisoner. Ed. Julia K. Jaffray. (Boston, Little, 1917). [Symposium of 14 contributors].

Prison Methods in New York State. PHILIP KLEIN. (London, King, 1920).

The American Prison System. JESSE P. WEBB. (Salem, Oregon, 1920).

Penology in the United States [contains bibliography]. L. N. ROBINSON. (Philadelphia, Winston, 1921).

Wall shadows: a study in American prisons [refers to about 70 American prisons]. FRANK TANNENBAUM. (New York, Putnam, 1922).

In the Clutch of Circumstances. A BURGLAR. (New York, Appleton, 1922).

Penology an Educational problem. H. H. HART. (New York, Russell Sage Foundation, 1923).

Crucibles of Crime: the shocking story of the American Jail. J. F. FISHMAN and V. PERLMAN. (New York, Cosmopolitan Press, 1923).

Historical Sketch of the indeterminate sentence and parole system. EDWARD LINDSEY. (*Journal of the American Institute of Criminal Law and Criminology*, Vol. XVI., 1925).

Prison Memories of an Anarchist [American Jails]. ALEX. BERKMAN. (C. W. Daniel, 1926).

Handbook of American Prisons and Reformatories [2 Federal and 11 State]. Ed. P. W. Garrett and A. H. McCormick. (National Society of Penal Information; New York, Putnam, 1925, 1929).

The Evolution of Penology in Pennsylvania: a study in American social history. H. E. BARNES. (Indianapolis, 1927).

American Prisons and Reformatory Institutions. M. LIEPMANN. (National Society for Mental Hygiene, 1928).

Man's Grim Justice [experiences of many American Jails]. JACK CALLAHAN. (John Long, 1929)

Life and Death in Sing Sing. LEWIS E. LAWES, Warden. (John Long, 1929).

Let To-morrow Come: Sketches of American Prison Life. A. J. BARR. (New York, 1929).

Prisons of To-morrow. (*Annals of American Academy of Political and Social Science,* Vol. CLVII., 1931).

Twenty Thousand Years in Sing Sing. LEWIS E. LAWES, Warden since 1929. (Constable, 1932).

Behind these Walls. [Reminiscences of life in an American prison]. JAMES R. WINNING. (John Long, 1933).

Sing Sing Doctor. AMOS O. SQUIRE [formerly chief physician at Sing Sing prison]. (Rich & Cowan, 1935).

AMERICA: ARGENTINA.

Sistema Penitenciario. J. INGEGNIEROS. (Buenos Aires, 1911).

G IV—PRISON STUDIES

G IV 1 — PRISON STUDIES BY EXECUTIVE OFFICERS.

Revelations of Prison Life with an enquiry into Prison Discipline and Secondary Punishments. G. L. CHESTERTON, Governor of House of Correction, Cold Bath Fields. 2 Vols. (Hurst & Blackett, 1856).

Female Life in Prison [Brixton and Millbank]. PRISON MATRON [F. W. ROBINSON]. 2 Vols. (Hurst & Blackett, 1862).

Prison characters drawn from life with suggestions for Prison Government. F. W. ROBINSON. (London; Spencer, Blackett, 1892).

Warder Cassidy on Prisons and Convicts: remarks from observations and experience gained during thirty seven years' continuous service in the administration of the Eastern State Penitentiary, Pennsylvania. M. J. CASSIDY. (Philadelphia; Patterson & White, 1897).

Fifty Years of Public Service [mainly Prison Service]. A. GRIFFITHS. (Cassell, 1904).

Fifty Years of Prison Service: an autobiography. T. R. BROCKWAY, Supt. of the Elmira Reformatory, 1876–1900. (New York, Charities Publication Committee, 1912).

Quod: Reminiscences of a Prison Governor. MAJOR WALLACE BLAKE. (Hodder & Stoughton, 1927).

Twenty Thousand Years in Sing Sing. LEWIS E. LAWES, Warden since 1920. (Constable, 1932).

Recollections of a Prison Governor [Wakefield, Northampton, Liverpool, Wandsworth, etc.]. LT.-COL. E. F. RICH. (Hurst & Blackett, 1932).

G IV 2 — PRISON STUDIES BY CHAPLAINS.

The advantages of a Separate System of imprisonment as at Reading. REV. JOHN FIELD, Chaplain, County Jail, Reading. (Longmans, 1846).

Chapters on Prisons and Prisoners. JOSEPH KINGSMILL, Chaplain, Islington Model Prison. (Longmans, 1854).

The Prison Chaplain: a Memoir of the Rev. John Clay, late Chaplain of Preston Jail. WALTER L. CLAY. (Cambridge; Macmillan, 1861).

Life among Convicts. CHARLES B. GIBSON, Chaplain in the Convict Service. (Hurst & Blackett, 1863).

Jottings from Jail: Notes and Papers on Prison Life. REV. J. W. HORSLEY, late Chaplain of H.M. Prison, Clerkenwell. (Fisher Unwin, 1887). [Includes valuable *Prison Calendar*, record of facts in prison history from A.D. 1394 to 1886].

Work among the Fallen as seen in the Prison Cell. REV. G. P. MERRICK. (Ward, Lock, 1891).

Prisons and Prisoners. REV. J. W. HORSLEY, late Chaplain, Clerkenwell Prison. (Pearson, 1898).

The Prison Cell in its Lights and Shadows. REV. JOHN PITKIN. (Sampson Low, 1918).

A Prison Chaplain on Dartmoor. REV. CLIFFORD RICKARDS. (Arnold, 1920).

Twenty-five years in six Prisons. EUSTACE JERVIS, Chaplain. [Wormwood Scrubs, Lewes, Portland, etc.]. Fisher Unwin, 1925).

G IV 3 — PRISON MEMOIRS BY INMATES. [*See also* B II 2].

Jail Journals or Five Years in British Prisons [Experiences at Bermuda, the Cape, and in Tasmania]. JOHN MITCHEL. (New York, Citizen Office, 1854; Glasgow, Cameron & Ferguson, 1876).

Impressions of Prison Life in Great Britain. D. DYER. (Albany, 1868).

Six Years in the Prisons of England [Scotland, Yorkshire, Surrey, etc.]. BY A. MERCHANT. Ed. F. Anderson. (London, Richard Bentley, 1868).

Five Years' Penal Servitude. BY ONE WHO HAS ENDURED IT. (London, Richard Bentley, 1878).

Convict Life, or Revelations concerning Convicts and Convict Prisons. BY A TICKET-OF-LEAVE MAN. (London, Wyman, 1879).

Eighteen months' Imprisonment, with a remissión. D[AVID] S[HAW], late Captain . . . . . . Regiment, (Routledge, 1883).

Twelve Months in an English Prison. SUSAN WILLIS FLETCHER. (Boston, U.S.A.; Lee & Shepard, 1884).

Leaves from a Prison Diary or Lectures to a Solitary Audience. MICHAEL DAVITT. 2 Vols. (Chapman & Hall, 1885).

I was in Prison. FREDERICK BROCKLEHURST. (F. Unwin, 1898).

Penal Servitude: a prisoners' own account [1897]. W.B.N. [Lord William Beauchamp Nevill]. (Heinemann, 1903).

Mark of the Broad Arrow or Life of a Convict. NO. 77. (Everett, 1903).

Twenty-five Years in Seventeen Prisons: the life history of an ex-convict, with his impressions of our Prison System. NO. 7 [pseud.]. (London; F. E. Robinson, 1903; Hutchinson, 1906).

My Prison Life [describes Holloway, Wormwood Scrubs, Portland, Pentonville, Parkhurst]. JABEZ S. BALFOUR. (Chapman & Hall, 1907).

A Holiday in Gaol. FREDERIC MARTYN. (Methuen, 1911).

Prison and Prisoners: some personal experiences of [Lady] Constance Lytton and Jane Warton, spinster [pseud.]. [Suffragette Movement]. (Heinemann, 1914).

Memories of Mountjoy [Dublin, 1915]. SEAN MILROY. (Dublin, Maunsel, 1917).

An English Prison from within. STEPHEN HOBHOUSE. (Allen & Unwin, 1919).

A Prisoner of Pentonville. RED BAND. (Elkin Matthews, 1920).

Glimpses of an Irish Felon's Prison Life. THOMAS J. CLARKE. (Dublin, Maunsel, 1922).

A Gentleman in Prison: Confessions written in Tokyo Prison. T. ISHII. Tr. by Caroline Macdonald. (London; Student Christian Movement, 1923).

Among the Broad Arrow Men. A plain account of English Prison Life. By B.2.15. (A. & C. Black, 1924).

Dartmoor from Within. JOCK of Parkhurst. (London, Newnes, 1931). JOCK of Dartmoor (Readers Library Pub. Co., 1933).

Shades of the Prison House: a personal memoir [of an ex-convict]. [Refers to Hull Prison, Maidstone, Parkhurst, Dartmoor, etc.]. STUART WOOD. (Williams Norgate, 1932).

The Lord High Executioner [prison experiences in England and America]. F. W. HARLAND-EDGECOMBE. (John Long, 1934).

I was a Prisoner [9 months in Yorkshire gaols]. WILLIAM HOLT. (Todmorden, John Miles, 1934).

G IV 4 — PRISON STUDIES BY OTHERS. [*See also* G III 1].

Essays and Characters of a Prison and Prisoners. GEOFFREY MYNSHULL. (1618; reprint, Edinburgh, W. C. Tait, 1821).

Thoughts on Prison Labour. STUDENT of the Inner Temple. [Plan of Cold Bath Fields Prison. Refers to use of treadmill]. (London, Rodwell & Martin, 1824).

Prison and Prisoners. JOSEPH ADSHEAD. (Longmans, 1845).

Our Convicts. MARY CARPENTER. 2 Vols. (Longmans, 1864). [Convict treatment; English convict system; transportation; disposal of criminals and ticket-of-leave; the Irish system].

Thirty years' experiences of a medical officer in the English Convict Service. J. CAMPBELL. (London, Nelsons, 1884).

Scenes from a Silent World; or Prisons and their Inmates. FRANCES SCOUGAL [pseud. *i.e.*, MISS F. M. F. SKENE]. (Blackwood, 1889, 1891).

Political Prisoners at Home and Abroad. DR. GEORGE SIGERSON. (Kegan Paul, 1890).

Sidelights on Convict Life. GEORGE C. GRIFFITH. (John Long, 1903).

Silent Gates: a voyage into Prison. TIGHE HOPKINS. (Herbert & Daniel, 1913).

Prison Reminiscences. HALF-TIMER. (London, Elliot Stock, 1917).

Prisons and Commonsense. T. M. OSBORNE. (Philadelphia, Lippincott, 1924).

The Human side of Crook and Convict Life [various interviews]. STANLEY SCOTT. (Hurst & Blackett, 1924).

His Majesty's Guests: Secrets of the Cells. 'WARDEN.' (Jarrolds, 1929).

The Prisoner and the Prison. SIR SIDNEY POCOCK [Visiting Magistrate to H.M. Prisons]. (Alston Rivers, 1930).

The Prisoner at the Bar [study of penal methods]. ARTHUR GARDNER [Prison Visitor]. (P. Allan, 1931).

The Prisoner's Soul — and our own. Experiences and observations from a prison in Oslo. BISHOP EIVIND BERGGRAV. Tr. by Laura Gravely. (Dent, 1932).

G V—PERIODICAL REPORTS

Great Britain and Ireland.

Report of the Commissioners of Prisons and Directors of Convict Prisons. [England and Wales]. (H.M.S.O.; annual).

Report of the Prisons Department for Scotland. (H.M.S.O.; annual).

Report of General Prisons Board [Irish Free State]. (Dublin; annual).

Reports on the work of the Children's Branch, Home Office. (H.M.S.O.; annual).

G VI—PERIODICAL LITERATURE DEVOTED TO PRISONS

England.

Howard Journal. (Howard League for Penal Reform, London; from 1921).

Tribunal; an international review of penal administration [in English, French and and German]. (Howard League for Penal Reform; from 1932).

The Penal Reformer. (Howard League for Penal Reform and National Council for the Abolition of the Death Penalty; from 1934).

France.

Revue pénitentiaire et de droit pénal. (Société Générale des Prisons, Paris; since 1877).

Germany.

Blätter für Gefängniskunde. (Verein der deutschen Strafanstaltsbeamten, Heidelberg; since 1865).

Italy.

Rivista di diritto penitenziario. (Rome, since 1930).

Poland.

Revue pénitentiaire de Pologne. (Warsaw; since 1927).

United States of America.

Prison Journal. (Pennsylvania Prison Society, Philadelphia; since 1921).

Bulletin. (National Society of Penal Information; New York).

H. REFORMATION

[The subject of REFORMATION is dealt with *passim* in Section G on Penology. JOHN HOWARD wrote: 'To reform prisoners ...... should always be the leading view of every house of correction.' The following includes some special literature].

H I—PROBATION [*See also* A V]

The Probation System in America. E. P. HUGHES. (London, Howard Association, 1903).

Memorandum on the Probation System as at present in force in the United States of America. Cmd. 3401. (H.M.S.O., 1907).

Probation of Offenders. Memorandum issued by the Home Secretary. (London, H.M.S.O., 1908).

Report of the Departmental Committee on the Probation of Offenders, 1907. Cmd. 5001. (H.M.S.O., 1909).

The Probation System. CECIL LEESON. (P.S. King, 1914).

Report of the Departmental Committee on the Training and Payment of Probation Officers. Cmd. 1601. (H.M.S.O., 1922).

Probation in Europe. T. W. TROUGHT, President of the National Association of Probation Officers. (Oxford, Blackwell, 1927). [In appendix gives details of Great Britain, Ireland and 12 European Countries].

Probation and Delinquency: the study and treatment of the individual delinquent. (New York, Catholic Charities of New York archdiocese, 1927).

Report of the Departmental Committee on the Treatment of Young Offenders. [H.M.S.O. 1927).

The Probation of offenders. H. H. AYSCOUGH. (W. J. Hewitt, 1929).

Probation and Criminal Justice. Ed. S. Glueck. (New York, Macmillan, 1933).

Juvenile Detention in the U.S.A.: a report of a field survey of the National Probation Association. FLORENCE M. WARNER. (Chicago University Press; Cambridge University Press, 1933).

Sparks beneath the Ashes: the experience of a London Probation Officer. MARY ELLISON. (Murray, 1934).

Juvenile Probation [Cases records of 500 children]. BELLE BOONE BEARD. (New York; American Book Co., 1934).

A Handbook of Probation and Social Work of the Courts. MRS. LE MESURIER. (London, National Association of Probation Officers, 47, Whitehall, S.W.1; 1935).

Directory of Probation Officers, Home Office Schools, Probation Hostels and Homes, and Borstal Institutions. (H.M.S.O.; annual).

H II—REFORMATORY SYSTEMS

Observations on penal institutions and the reformation of criminals. WILLIAM ROSCOE. (Cadell, 1819).

Reformatory Schools for the children of the Perishing and Dangerous Classes and for Juvenile Offenders. MARY CARPENTER. (Gilpin, 1851).

Reformatory Education: papers on preventive, correctional and reformatory institutions and agencies in different countries. H. BARNARD. (Hartford, Mass., U.S.A., 1857).

The New York State Reformatory in Elmira. ALEX. WINTER. (Sonnenschein, 1891).

Papers relating to the transfer of the Control of Reformatory Schools in India from the Jail Department to the Education Department during the year 1898–99. (Government of India, Home Department, Selection, No. 376).

The Reformatory System in the United States. S. J. BARROWS. (U.S. House Document 459, 56th Congress, 1st Session, Washington, U.S.A., 1900).

Administration and educational work of American Juvenile Reformatories. D. SNEDDEN. (Columbia University, New York, 1907).

Das moderne amerikainsche besserungs-system. PAUL HERR. (Berlin, Kohlhammer, 1907).

Young Delinquents. a study of Reformatory and Industrial Schools. MARY G. BARNETT. (Methuen, 1913).

The Making of Men. J. W. COOMBES, Supt., Chingleput Reformatory School, Madras Presidency, India. (Seeley, Service, 1920).

Romance of Child Reformation. M. [later SIR MEYER] A. SPIELMAN, H.M. Inspector of Reformatory and Industrial Schools. (London, Reformatory and Refuge Union, 1920).

The American State Reformatory, with special reference to its educational aspects. FRANK F. NALDER. (Berkeley, University of California Press, 1920).

Reformatory Reform. ISAAC G. BRIGGS. (Longmans, 1924).

Reformatories for Women in the United States. EUGENIA C. LEKKERKERKER. (Groningen, J. B. Wolters, 1931).

Report of the Departmental Committee on the Employment of Prisoners. Pt. II. Employment on Discharge. [Deals with Prisoners' Aid Societies and other After-Care organizations]. (Cmd. 4897 ; H.M.S.O., 1935).

H III—BORSTAL SYSTEM

Borstal in 1910: Account of Borstal and the Borstal Association. (London, The Borstal Association, 15, Buckingham Street, Strand, 1910).

The Principles of Borstal Treatment as applied to Indian Prisons. CAPT. FREDERIC A. BARKER. (Lahore, 1915).

The Truth about Borstal. SYDNEY A. MOSELEY. (Cecil Palmer, 1926).

Notes on Imprisonment, Borstal Detention. (H.M.S.O., 1928).

Borstalians : the First Authentic Account of Life at a Borstal Institution by a Borstal Boy. J. W. GORDON. (Martin Hopkinson, 1932).

The English Borstal System : a study in the treatment of young offenders. S. BARMAN. (King, 1934). [Contains bibliography].

J. CONNECTED ASSOCIATIONS, CONGRESSES AND SOCIETIES.

[For Periodicals, *see* Subject Index.]

Howard Association for the Promotion of the best methods of Treatment and Prevention of Crime, Pauperism, etc., from 1895 to 1920. Published *The Howard Journal*, London.

Penal Reform League, from 1907 to 1920.

Howard League for Penal Reform [Founded 1921]. Parliament Mansions, Orchard Street, Victoria Street, S.W.1, London.

Reformatory and Refuge Union [Founded 1856]. 17, Leigham Court Road, S.W.16, London.

Medico-Legal Society [Founded 1901]. 11, Chandos Street, W.1, London.

Institute for the Scientific Treatment of Delinquency [Founded 1932]. 56, Grosvenor Street, W.1., London.

National Council for the Abolition of the Death Penalty. (Parliament Mansions, Orchard Street, London, S.W.1).

National Society of Penal Information. (New York ; publishes Bulletin).

Borstal Association, 131, Victoria Street, S.W.1, London.

National Association of Probation Officers, 47, Whitehall, S.W.1, London.

Aylesbury After-Care Association. Aylesbury.

International Criminal Police Commission. First, Vienna, 1923. Second Vienna, 1924. Third, Berlin, 1926. Fourth, Amsterdam, 1927. Fifth, Berne, 1928. Sixth, Vienna, 1930. Seventh, Antwerp, 1930. Eighth, Paris, 1931. Ninth, Rome, 1932. Tenth, Vienna, 1934. (Police Headquarters, Vienna.)

Organ :—*International Oeffentliche Sicherheit* (Deutschmeisterplatz 3, Vienna ; fortnightly).

American Institute of Criminal Law and Criminology [Founded 1909], 357, E. Chicago Avenue, Chicago.

Organ :—*Journal of the American Institute of Criminal Law and Criminology*, Northwestern University Law Publishing Association, Chicago, U.S.A., since 1910.

International Prison Congress (Congrès Pénitentiaire International). First, London, 1872. Second, Stockholm, 1878. Third, Rome, 1885. Fourth, St. Petersburg, 1890. Fifth, Berne, 1895. Sixth, Brussels, 1900. Seventh, Budapest, 1905. Eighth, Washington, 1910. Ninth, London, 1925. Tenth, Prague, 1930. Eleventh, Berlin, 1935 (Congrès Pénal et Pénitentiaire International).

Standing Committee :—*International Penal and Penitentiary Commission.* Secretary General, Berne, Switzerland.

American Prison Association [Founded 1870], 135 East 15th Street, New York City. Congress held annually.

National Association of Prison Visitors. Hon. Sec., 79, Queen Street, E.C.4, London.

Royal Society for the Assistance of Discharged Prisoners, 44, Burton Street, W.C.1, London. [60 other Societies throughout England and Scotland].

Central Discharged Prisoners' Aid Society [Founded 1878]. Victory House, Leicester Square, W.C.2, London.

Central Association for the Aid of Discharged Convicts. [Founded 1911]. 131, Victoria Street, S.W.1, London.

Foreign Organisations for the assistance of discharged prisoners.

AMERICA. Many local Associations ; *e.g., Massachusetts Society for aiding discharged prisoners*, Boston, State House.

BELGIUM. *Commission royale de patronage et de reclassement des détenus libérés.*

FRANCE. *Union des Sociétés de patronage des détenus libérés*, Place Dauphine 14, Paris.

GERMANY. *Deutscher Reichszusammens schluss für gerichtshilfe, Gefangenen- und entlassenenfürsorge der freien Wohlfahrtspflege.*

HOLLAND. *Nederlandsch Genootschap tot Zedelijke Verbetering der Gevangenen.*

ITALY. Official body under the Minister of Justice.

International Congress for the assistance of Discharged Prisoners: published proceedings *:*

Antwerp, 1890. (Brussels, Guyot, 1891).

Antwerp, 1894. (Brussels, Brouwers & Fils, 1895).

Antwerp, 1898. (No publication).

Liege, 1905. (Brussels, J. Gormare, 1907).

Antwerp, 1911. (Antwerp, J. Kennes fils, 1911).

K. BIBLIOGRAPHIES

dealing with certain aspects of crime and cognate subjects are to be found in the following works, which are arranged in the order of date of publication.

Lehrbuch der Gefängniskunde. [Contains regional bibliographies for England and Continental countries]. K. KROHNE. (Stuttgart, 1889).

An Introduction to the Study of Dependent, Defective and Delinquent Classes and of their social treatment. PROF. C. R. HENDERSON. (Boston, U.S.A., D. C. Heath, 1893, 1901).

Abnormal Man. A. MACDONALD. (Washington, U.S.A., Lowdermilk, 1893).

Criminology. A. MACDONALD. (New York ; Funk & Wagnalls, 1893).

The Criminal. A. DRÄHMS. (New York, Macmillan, 1900).

Crime in its relation to social progress. A. C. HALL. (New York, Macmillan, 1902).

Recent Object Lessons in Penal Science. A. R. WHITEWAY. (Third series ; Sonnenschein, 1902).

La Sociologie Criminelle. E. FERRI. Tr. by Ferrier from Italian. (Paris, 1905).

Criminal Investigation. DR. HANS GROSS. (Specialist Press, 1907).

The London Police Court. H. R. P. GAMON. (Dent, 1907).

Juvenile Crime and Reformation. ARTHUR MACDONALD. (Washington Government Printing Office, 1908).

A Systematical List of the Principal Works on Criminal Law and Criminology. (The Hague, M. Nijhoff, 1909).

A Preliminary Bibliography of Modern Criminal Law and Criminology. JOHN H. WIGMORE. (Chicago, Northwestern University, 1909). [Consists of an author index of about 3,000 entries, in five languages].

Criminal Man. C. LOMBROSO and G. L. FERRERO. (Putnam, 1911).

List of Works relating to Criminology. (New York Public Library, V.15 ; New York, 1911).

Criminal Psychology. DR. HANS GROSS. (Heinemann, 1911).

Select List of References on Capital Punishment. HERMANN H. B. MEYER. (Washington, U.S.A. ; Government Printing Office, 1912).

The Best Books. W. S. SONNENSCHEIN. [References to Criminology, Penology, Police, Prisons]. (Routledge, 1912).

The Individual Delinquent. DR. WILLIAM HEALY. (Heinemann, 1915).

List of References on Prison Labor. HERMANN H. B. MEYER. (Washington, U.S.A. ; Government Printing Office, 1915).

Capital Punishment in the United States. RAYMOND T. BYE. (Philadelphia, 1919).

The Literature of Crime. COLIN A. MACPHERSON, Indian Police. (Lahore, C. & M. Gazette, 1919).

Penology in the United States. L. N. ROBINSON. (Philadelphia, Winston, 1921).

English Prisons of To-day. Appendix IV. S. HOBHOUSE and A. F. BROCKWAY. (Longmans, 1922).

List of References on Crime and Criminology in the United States with special reference to statistics. (United States Library of Congress, Division of Bibliography ; Washington, 1922).

List of References on juvenile courts and probation in the United States and a selected list of foreign references. Children's Bureau No. 124. (Washington ; Government Printing Office, 1923).

Insanity and the Criminal. JOHN C. GOODWIN. (Hutchinson, 1923).

Single Finger Print System. J. A. LARSON. (New York, Appleton, 1924).

Selected articles on Capital Punishment Ed. Lamar T. Beman. (New York, Wilson, 1925).

The Young Delinquent. CYRIL BURT. (University of London Press, 1925).

A Bibliography on probation, juvenile . . . courts, crime, etc. (New York, National Probation Association, 1926).

A Guide to Material on Crime and Criminal Justice. A. F. KUHLMAN. (New York, Social Science Research Council ; H. W. Wilson Company, 1929). [Contains 13,276 entries, minutely classified and taken from 13 American libraries ; but is limited to material published in the United States up to 1927].

La Rôle des Laboratoires de police technique. MOHAMMED ZAKI. (Lyons, Desvigne, 1929).

Crime and Criminal Law in the United States. HARRY BEST. (New York, Macmillan, 1930).

Criminology. Art. in *Encyclopædia of the Social Sciences,* Vol. IV. H. E. BARNES. (Macmillan, 1931).

Questioned Documents. ALBERT S. OSBORN. (Sweet & Maxwell, 1931).

Crime. Art. in *Encyclopædia of the Social Sciences,* Vol. IV. THORSTEN SELLIN. (Macmillan, 1931).

The Crime of Punishment. MARGARET WILSON. (J. Cape, 1931).

A Brief Guide to Penological Literature. T. SELLIN. (Chicago, *Annals of the American Academy of Political and Social Science,* Vol. CLVII., p. 225–232 ; 1931).

Bibliography on Police Organization and Administration, Criminal Identification and Investigation. AUGUSTE VOLLMER. (Chicago, *American Journal of Police Science,* Vol. II., p. 76 ; 1931).

Catalogue of the John Howard Library of Criminal Law and Penology. (London, Howard League for Penal Reform, 1931). [Addenda to 1934].

A London Bibliography of the Social Sciences. B. HEADICAR and C. FULLER. 4 Vols. (London School of Economics ; London, 1931, 1932). [References to Crime, Police and Prisons].

From Punishment to Prevention. PROSANTO KUMAR SEN. (Oxford University Press, 1932).

A History of Capital Punishment. JOHN LAURENCE. (Sampson Low, 1932).

London Prisons of to-day and yesterday. ALBERT CREW. [22 items]. (Nicholson & Watson, 1933).

Traité de Criminalistique. E. LOCARD. (Lyons, Desvigne, 1933).

Police. Art. in *Encyclopædia of the Social Sciences,* Vol. XII. BRUCE SMITH. (Macmillan, 1934).

The English Borstal System. S. BARMAN. (P.S. King, 1934).

The Modern English Prison. L. W. FOX. (Routledge, Kegan Paul, 1934).

Penal Institutions. Art. in *Encyclopædia of the Social Sciences,* Vol. XII. THORSTEN SELLIN. (Macmillan, 1934).

Bibliography of Crime and Criminal Justice, 1927-31 [13,292 entries]. DOROTHY C. CULVER. (Calif. Univ. Bureau of Public Administration, New York, Wilson, 1934). [Continuation of Kuhlman's *Guide,* 1929].

Bibliography of the Training of Police. D. CAMPBELL. (Chicago ; *Journal of the American Institute of Criminal Law and Criminology,* Vol. XXIV., p. 591 ; 1933-34).

Criminology. ALBERT MORRIS. (Longmans, 1935). [Elaborate ; under various heads ; chiefly American publications].

ADDITIONS

A III 1 — STUDIES OF CRIME : GREAT BRITAIN.

Crime. Chap. XII. of 'Life and Leisure', being Vol. IX. of 'The New Survey of London Life and Labour'. S. K. RUCK. (P. S. King, 1935).

A IV 3 — CRIMINAL STATISTICS.

Criminal Statistics as a Guide to Police Efficiency. R. G. B. SPICER, Insp. Gen., Palestine Police. (*Police Journal*, vol. vii ; p. 209, April, 1934).

B I 1 — CRIMINALS : COLLECTIONS.

The Black Maria, or the Criminals' Omnibus. Conducted by HARRY HODGE. (Gollancz and William Hodge, 1935). [Collections of editorial introductions to 15 cases from F II 1].

B III 1 — STUDIES : MURDER.

Memoirs of a London County Coroner [includes various murder cases and an analysis of the law relating to murder]. DR. H. R. OSWALD. (Stanley Paul, 1935).

C II — HISTORY OF POLICE FORCES : THAMES RIVER POLICE.

The Thames Police. Supt. H. DALTON, Ex-Chief Insp., Thames Division, Metropolitan Police. (*Police Journal*, vol. viii, p. 90 ; Jan., 1935).

D II 3 — POLICE ADMINISTRATION : METROPOLITAN AREA.

The Story of Scotland Yard. SIR BASIL THOMSON. (Grayson, 1935).

E II 7 — DETECTION : FORENSIC MEDICINE.

Forensic Medicine. DR. DOUGLAS KERR, Police Surgeon, Edinburgh. (A. & C. Black, 1935).

E III 1 — DETECTION : ENGLAND.

I Guarded Kings ; the Memoirs of a Political Police Officer. EX-DET. INSP. HAROLD BRUST. (Stanley Paul, 1935).

F I — TRIALS : COLLECTIONS.

When Justice Faltered [studies of 9 murder trials]. RICHARD S. LAMBERT. (Methuen, 1935).

G III 2 (*c*) — PENAL INSTITUTIONS : GERMANY.

The Prison System of Germany. [Prepared for the 11th International Penal and Penitentiary Congress]. (Berlin, Reich Ministry of Justice, 1935).

K — BIBLIOGRAPHIES.

Modern Criminal Investigation. H. SÖDERMAN and J. J. O'CONNELL. (New York, Funk, 1935). [202 entries ; mostly foreign].

COMBINED SUBJECT
AND
GEOGRAPHICAL INDEX

AUTHOR INDEX.

ed.—Editor. *trans.*—Translator. *pseud.*—Pseudonym.

Patterson Smith Reprint Series in
Criminology, Law Enforcement, and Social Problems

1. Lewis: *The Development of American Prisons and Prison Customs, 1776-1845*
2. Carpenter: *Reformatory Prison Discipline*
3. Brace: *The Dangerous Classes of New York*
4. Dix: *Remarks on Prisons and Prison Discipline in the United States*
5. Bruce *et al: The Workings of the Indeterminate-Sentence Law and the Parole System in Illinois*
6. Wickersham Commission: *Complete Reports, Including the Mooney-Billings Report.* 14 Vols.
7. Livingston: *Complete Works on Criminal Jurisprudence.* 2 Vols.
8. Cleveland Foundation: *Criminal Justice in Cleveland*
9. Illinois Association for Criminal Justice: *The Illinois Crime Survey*
10. Missouri Association for Criminal Justice: *The Missouri Crime Survey*
11. Aschaffenburg: *Crime and Its Repression*
12. Garofalo: *Criminology*
13. Gross: *Criminal Psychology*
14. Lombroso: *Crime, Its Causes and Remedies*
15. Saleilles: *The Individualization of Punishment*
16. Tarde: *Penal Philosophy*
17. McKelvey: *American Prisons*
18. Sanders: *Negro Child Welfare in North Carolina*
19. Pike: *A History of Crime in England.* 2 Vols.
20. Herring: *Welfare Work in Mill Villages*
21. Barnes: *The Evolution of Penology in Pennsylvania*
22. Puckett: *Folk Beliefs of the Southern Negro*
23. Fernald *et al: A Study of Women Delinquents in New York State*
24. Wines: *The State of the Prisons and of Child-Saving Institutions*
25. Raper: *The Tragedy of Lynching*
26. Thomas: *The Unadjusted Girl*
27. Jorns: *The Quakers as Pioneers in Social Work*
28. Owings: *Women Police*
29. Woolston: *Prostitution in the United States*
30. Flexner: *Prostitution in Europe*
31. Kelso: *The History of Public Poor Relief in Massachusetts: 1820-1920*
32. Spivak: *Georgia Nigger*
33. Earle: *Curious Punishments of Bygone Days*
34. Bonger: *Race and Crime*
35. Fishman: *Crucibles of Crime*
36. Brearley: *Homicide in the United States*
37. Graper: *American Police Administration*
38. Hichborn: *"The System"*
39. Steiner & Brown: *The North Carolina Chain Gang*
40. Cherrington: *The Evolution of Prohibition in the United States of America*
41. Colquhoun: *A Treatise on the Commerce and Police of the River Thames*
42. Colquhoun: *A Treatise on the Police of the Metropolis*
43. Abrahamsen: *Crime and the Human Mind*
44. Schneider: *The History of Public Welfare in New York State: 1609-1866*
45. Schneider & Deutsch: *The History of Public Welfare in New York State: 1867-1940*
46. Crapsey: *The Nether Side of New York*
47. Young: *Social Treatment in Probation and Delinquency*
48. Quinn: *Gambling and Gambling Devices*
49. McCord & McCord: *Origins of Crime*
50. Worthington & Topping: *Specialized Courts Dealing with Sex Delinquency*

Patterson Smith Reprint Series in
Criminology, Law Enforcement, and Social Problems

51. Asbury: *Sucker's Progress*
52. Kneeland: *Commercialized Prostitution in New York City*
53. Fosdick: *American Police Systems*
54. Fosdick: *European Police Systems*
55. Shay: *Judge Lynch: His First Hundred Years*
56. Barnes: *The Repression of Crime*
57. Cable: *The Silent South*
58. Kammerer: *The Unmarried Mother*
59. Doshay: *The Boy Sex Offender and His Later Career*
60. Spaulding: *An Experimental Study of Psychopathic Delinquent Women*
61. Brockway: *Fifty Years of Prison Service*
62. Lawes: *Man's Judgment of Death*
63. Healy & Healy: *Pathological Lying, Accusation, and Swindling*
64. Smith: *The State Police*
65. Adams: *Interracial Marriage in Hawaii*
66. Halpern: *A Decade of Probation*
67. Tappan: *Delinquent Girls in Court*
68. Alexander & Healy: *Roots of Crime*
69. Healy & Bronner: *Delinquents and Criminals*
70. Cutler: *Lynch-Law*
71. Gillin: *Taming the Criminal*
72. Osborne: *Within Prison Walls*
73. Ashton: *The History of Gambling in England*
74. Whitlock: *On the Enforcement of Law in Cities*
75. Goldberg: *Child Offenders*
76. Cressey: *The Taxi-Dance Hall*
77. Riis: *The Battle with the Slum*
78. Larson *et al: Lying and Its Detection*
79. Comstock: *Frauds Exposed*
80. Carpenter: *Our Convicts.* 2 Vols. in 1
81. Horn: *Invisible Empire: The Story of the Ku Klux Klan, 1866-1871*
82. Faris *et al: Intelligent Philanthropy*
83. Robinson: *History and Organization of Criminal Statistics in the United States*
84. Reckless: *Vice in Chicago*
85. Healy: *The Individual Delinquent*
86. Bogen: *Jewish Philanthropy*
87. Clinard: *The Black Market: A Study of White Collar Crime*
88. Healy: *Mental Conflicts and Misconduct*
89. Citizens' Police Committee: *Chicago Police Problems*
90. Clay: *The Prison Chaplain*
91. Peirce: *A Half Century with Juvenile Delinquents*
92. Richmond: *Friendly Visiting Among the Poor*
93. Brasol: *Elements of Crime*
94. Strong: *Public Welfare Administration in Canada*
95. Beard: *Juvenile Probation*
96. Steinmetz: *The Gaming Table.* 2 Vols.
97. Crawford: *Report on the Pentitentiaries of the United States*
98. Kuhlman: *A Guide to Material on Crime and Criminal Justice*
99. Culver: *Bibliography of Crime and Criminal Justice: 1927-1931*
100. Culver: *Bibliography of Crime and Criminal Justice: 1932-1937*